2004 St Nicholas Day

D1500235

For the
most wonderful
and beautiful
girl in the
world ♡

JOYFULLY LIVING THE GOSPEL
DAY BY DAY

"I have revealed these things to you so that My joy may be in you and your joy may be complete" (John 15:11).

JOYFULLY LIVING THE GOSPEL DAY BY DAY

MINUTE MEDITATIONS FOR EVERY DAY CONTAINING A SCRIPTURE READING, A REFLECTION, AND A PRAYER

By
FATHER JOHN CATOIR

Illustrated

CATHOLIC BOOK PUBLISHING CO.
New Jersey

CONTENTS

NIHIL OBSTAT: Sr. Kathleen Flanagan, S.C., Ph.D.
Censor Librorum

IMPRIMATUR: ✛ Frank J. Rodimer, J.C.D.
Bishop of Paterson

The Nihil Obstat and Imprimatur are official declarations that a book or a pamphlet is free of doctrinal or moral error. No implication is contained therein that those who have granted the Nihil Obstat and Imprimatur agree with the contents, opinions or statements expressed.

(T-188)

INTRODUCTION

S T. Paul defined joy as one of the fruits of the Holy Spirit: *"The fruits of the Spirit are charity, joy, peace . . ."* (Gal 5:22).

The word fruit is used to denote the end-product of a process, or the result of some prior disposition. Joy is the by-product of a life lived under the inspiration of the Holy Spirit rather than a prize attained in some kind of competition.

Joy is the by-product of our intimacy with the indwelling Trinity. Jesus leads us to this life. Remember His words at the Last Supper, *"I have revealed these things to you so that . . . your joy may be complete"* (Jn 15:11).

The words of Jesus continually point us in the direction of joy.

"Have confidence, be of good cheer," says the Lord, "in this world you will have many troubles, but I have overcome the world" (Jn 16:33).

Listening to the Word of God in a spirit of obedience will transform you into a new creation. Faith is not merely a matter of pious devotions; faith involves a willingness to obey.

"If you love Me, and obey Me, I will ask the Father and He will give you another Comforter, and He will never leave you" (Jn 14:15, 16).

This Comforter is none other than the Holy Spirit of joy, peace, and love. Genuine faith, therefore, hears the words of Jesus and takes them to heart.

That means that if Jesus says "Cheer up," you must try to snap yourself out of the blues. How does one do that? By guarding your mind from negative thinking. This little book will help you fine-tune your thinking. If Jesus says, *"Be not afraid,"* (Lk 12:4), then cancel those dreadful thoughts that cause you so much inner distress. The first step after belief is obedience.

Bl. Juliana of Norwich wrote these inspired words, "The greatest honor we can give to Almighty God, greater than all our sacrifices and mortifications, is to live gladly, joyfully, because of the knowledge of His love."

You can do this. You can think of the good you have done, not the bad, the love you have received not the hate, the laughter you have shared not the tears. You can focus on God's unchanging Love and be grateful in all circumstances. It pleases God to see you enjoy your precious life.

"Ask and you will receive, so that your joy may be complete" (Jn 16:24).

Pursue a love-filled life, and joy will surely follow.

Joy is the infallible sign of the presence of the Holy Spirit.

"Rejoice with those who rejoice; weep with those who weep. Live in harmony with one another. Do not consider yourself to be better than others, but associate with the lowly, and do not consider yourself to be wiser than you are" (Rom 12:15).

I hope this book brings you hours of quiet enjoyment. Meanwhile, it is my prayer that the Lord will truly be your strength and your joy.

Father John Catoir

ARY said, "Behold the handmaid of the Lord. May it be done to me according to your word."

JAN. 1

—Lk 1:38

REFLECTION. Mary, the Mother of the Church, is also called the Cause for our Joy. Pope John Paul II explains why:

"Christ came to bring joy: joy to children, joy to parents, joy to families and friends, joy to workers, and to scholars, joy to the sick and elderly, joy to all humanity. In a true sense joy is the keynote message and the recurring motif of the Gospels. . . . Be messengers of joy."

PRAYER. *Lord Jesus, teach me to be joyful on this, the first day of the year, and on all the days of my life.*

LESSED are we, O Israel, for what pleases God is known to us.

JAN. 2

—Bar 4:4

REFLECTION. Love and good cheer go together. More than a century ago, Thomas Carlyle, the English historian, said: "Wondrous is the strength of cheerfulness and its power of endurance. The cheerful man will do more in the same time, will do it better, will persevere in it longer, than the sad or sullen."

Good cheer is universally praised.

PRAYER. *Help me, Lord of my heart, to be of good cheer. I know that You love a cheerful giver, and I have a long way to go.*

REJOICE in the Lord always. Again I say: Rejoice. . . . The Lord is near. Do not worry about anything. —Phil 4:4-5

JAN. 3

REFLECTION. The challenge of Paul has always intrigued me. Not only does he tell us not to worry about anything, he tells us to rejoice—always.

It seems a bit far-fetched when you consider the problems he was enduring himself. Here was a man facing trial and the danger of bodily punishment. He was flogged and imprisoned, but still he calls us to be joyful.

PRAYER. *Father in heaven, teach me how to reject my fears, that I may live in Your joy.*

THE person who is without love does not know God, for God is love. —1 Jn 4:8

JAN. 4

REFLECTION. Love is a basket of bread
from which to eat
for years to come.
Good loaves
fragrant and warm
miraculously multiplied;
the basket is never empty
the bread never stale.

—*Catherine de Vinck*

PRAYER. *Heavenly Lord, increase my love, and my joy.*

8

BUT above all these things have charity, which is the bond of perfection.

—Col 3:14

JAN.

5

REFLECTION. Dear Lord, You bless everyone with the ability to love. To know You is to love You. To love You is to rejoice with You.

Still there are those who do not show signs of knowing You, the one, true God. Millions have not encountered Your Son, Jesus.

PRAYER. *Jesus, help me to be a carrier of Your love. Show me the way to make Your Name known and loved.*

AND this is love, that we walk according to His commandments.

—1 Jn 5:3

JAN.

6

REFLECTION. Christ declared, "No one comes to the Father except through Me" (Jn 14:6).

The human heart longs for love. Without love, there is no joy. If you really love, you will be willing to make sacrifices. Joy and surrender go hand in hand.

PRAYER. *I love You, my Lord, and my God. Teach me to love You more and more, that my joy may be full.*

9

GIVE thanks to the Lord, for He is good; for His mercy endures forever. —Dan 3:89

JAN. 7

REFLECTION. Ten lepers approached Jesus as He was traveling to Jerusalem. People shunned them and feared them, because of the danger of contagion. Christ was moved to pity. He told them to visit the priests of the Mosaic Law, who would judge their cleansing.

All ten were miraculously cured. Only one returned to give thanks. Jesus said to him, "Your faith has saved you" (Lk 17:19).

PRAYER. *Thank You, Lord, for giving me peace of mind and heart. I rejoice in Your love.*

OUR heart shall rejoice, and your limbs shall flourish like the young grass. The power of the Lord shall be made known to His servants. —Isa 66:14

JAN. 8

REFLECTION. All of us are seeking the same thing: happiness. We have so much in common. Even though we may have traveled different roads to reach our present state in life, our basic hope is the same: a brighter, happier future.

We would all like to believe the future will be better than anything we have ever known before. The fact is, with the help of God, it will be.

PRAYER. *Father, let Your Light shine in me, that I may give peace and joy to others.*

EVERYONE who hears these words of Mine and acts in accordance with them will be like a wise man who constructed his house on a rock foundation. —Mt 7:24

JAN. 9

REFLECTION. The words of the Lord give wisdom and life. If you are willing to lose your life for the sake of the Kingdom, you will gain it for eternity.

Surrendering oneself is never easy. We know that it is in giving that we receive, but we do not easily grasp the idea that it is in dying that we are born to eternal life.

PRAYER. *Dear Jesus, thank You for guiding me through the narrow gate that leads to a joyful life. Teach me that the secret of joy resides in trusting Your promises.*

 WISDOM is glorious and never fades away, and is easily seen by those who love her, and found by those who seek her. —Wis 6:13

JAN. 10

REFLECTION. You have within you everything that you need to purchase the Kingdom of Heaven.

Joy will be purchased by your sorrow, rest by your labor, glory by your humiliation, and eternal life by your passing death.

— *St. Augustine*

PRAYER. *Dear Lord, we reap what we sow. Give me the wisdom to know how to draw joy from sorrow.*

N His love and in His mercy He redeemed them, and He carried them and lifted them up. —Isa 63:9

JAN. 11

REFLECTION. To be lifted up in the joy of the Lord is an experience we might call a mystical grace. Perhaps such moments are more common than we think.

There are times when you feel God's love deeply, and other times you feel nothing. In these matters feelings are not facts. God is always loving you.

PRAYER. *Teach me, Lord, that You are Unchanging Love, no matter what I might be feeling at any given moment.*

 ONSIDER it joy when you fall into various trials, knowing that the testing of your faith begets perseverance. —Jas 1:2-3

JAN. 12

REFLECTION. Joy is possible even in difficult circumstances. Joy is nothing like the happiness of a fun time; rather it is more a deep inner contentment, which comes from the knowledge of God's love.

PRAYER. *Jesus, my Lord and my God, what joy I feel when I know I have done something to please You. Help me when I am not so sure of myself. It is difficult to believe that Your love does not depend on my good behavior. You love the sinner even before he repents.*

12

IF someone forces you to go one mile, go with him for a second mile.

—Mt 5:41

REFLECTION. Bearing wrongs patiently goes with the challenge to love. Getting even is not permitted.

The words of the crucified Christ echo down from His Cross: "Father, forgive them for they do not know what they are doing" (Lk 23:34).

PRAYER. *Dear Jesus, You are my defender and guardian. You are my shield in the battle of life. In You I put my trust.*

NEITHER death, nor life . . . can separate us from the love of God, which is in Christ Jesus.   —Rom 8:38-39

REFLECTION. The Love of God is constant and unchanging. Nothing can stop God from loving because it is His nature to love. God loves us all equally.

Like the rain falling in a forest, on various trees and flowers, God's love falls on everyone of us in exactly the same way.

PRAYER. *Jesus, Your love is the Good News of the Gospel. Help me to relax and enjoy it.*

I F anyone teaches otherwise . . . he is proud, dwelling on questions and disputes of words. —1 Tim 6:3-4

15

REFLECTION. The Humanist Creed was first codified in 1933 when American humanists, under the leadership of John Dewey, philosopher and educator, drew up the "Humanist Manifesto."

The Manifesto was loaded with hostility against traditional religion. It held that there is no God; that religious belief is an enemy of human progress, and that only rationality and science can save us.

PRAYER. *Deliver me, O Lord, from the darkness of false teaching. Let me know the joy of loving You with all my heart.*

T HE Lord looks upon those who love Him; He is their shield and support. —Sir 34:16

JAN.
16

REFLECTION. I am sure of God's hand and guidance. . . . I am thankful to go the way by which I am being led.

My past life is full of God's mercy. Above all sin stands the forgiving love of the Crucified. —*Dietrich Bonhoeffer*

PRAYER. *Thank You, Lord, for protecting me in my hour of need. How blessed I am to know that You are always with me.*

T is my wish that you be free of all anxieties. —1 Cor 7:32

JAN. 17

REFLECTION. We must be convinced of the necessity of having a living, authentic, and active faith. That is all the more true today, when we face so many difficulties.

It is not enough to have a vague, weak, or uncertain faith. —*Pope John XXIII*

PRAYER. *O Lord, I often feel like the man in the Gospels who asked You to help what little faith he had. Fill my heart with Your gift of faith; let my faith be active and living.*

F you have faith like a mustard seed, you will say to this mountain, "Move from here"; and it will move. —Mt 17:19

JAN. 18

REFLECTION. The gift of faith is the most basic gift of the Holy Spirit because it opens us to a new level of strength and joy.

It is said that where your treasure is there your heart will also be. Even if you have only a tiny bit of faith, it will be enough to move mountains.

PRAYER. *Lord, I believe; help me in my unbelief. Give me a certain, untroubled faith in Your love.*

15

THOSE who sow in tears shall reap in joy.
—Ps 126:5

REFLECTION. Grace is the force within us that pulls us to safety. As we plod along in search of holiness we are saved again and again, and we ourselves become capable of helping others along the way.

". . . All those who give themselves to the struggle for the redemption of the world from greed, cruelty, injustice, selfish desire and their results—find themselves supported and reinforced by a spiritual power which enhances life, strengthens will, and purifies character" (Evelyn Underhill).

PRAYER. *Dearest Lord, I know that the work of transformation in the Spirit takes time. Teach me to be patient.*

BLESSED be God, Who has not rejected my prayer, nor withdrawn His mercy from me.
—Ps 66:20

REFLECTION. Open your mind, your heart, and your soul to God.

Open yourself to the infinity of Divine love.

PRAYER. *Holy Spirit, soul of my soul, I adore You; comfort me, console me. Let me know Your Will, and give me the courage to follow it.*

W HOEVER humbles himself and becomes like this little child is the greatest in the Kingdom of Heaven. —Mt 18:4

JAN. 21

REFLECTION. We are given freedom, but we do not always know how to use it. Being only dimly aware of the power and the mystery of evil, we are like blind children playing near the cliff's edge.

God's answer to our dilemma is grace. Grace saves us from ourselves.

PRAYER. *Dear Lord, I know that Your grace is sufficient for me. Help me to forgive myself when I go astray, and not be too hard on myself. Help me to understand that the Saints were not Saints 24 hours a day every day.*

T HOSE who wish to be My disciples must deny themselves, take up their cross daily, and follow Me. —Lk 9:23

JAN. 22

REFLECTION. The things that are going badly, are the work of the devil, and that is why I prefer you not to have too many scruples about your sins.

Think of them only so as to see God's forgiveness. —*Archbishop de Provencheres*

PRAYER. *Dear Lord, raise me up, and give me courage that I may carry my cross bravely.*

HIS cup is the New Covenant in My Blood. Do this, as often as you drink it, in remembrance of Me.

JAN. **23**

—1 Cor 11:25

REFLECTION. To look at the Lord in His Agony on the Cross is to come to this realization:

He will go to any extent to save those whom He loves.

PRAYER. *Lord, You are the source of my confidence and hope. Help me to put my trust in You fully. Thank You for the Eucharist that nourishes me day by day.*

 OU are now in anguish, but I will see you again, and your hearts will rejoice.

JAN. **24**

—Jn 16:22

REFLECTION. Those who turn to the Lord in difficult times, delight Him. He wants to carry your cross with you. He wants to become your Simon of Cyrene. His service is freely given.

Dispose your soul for an increase of grace because every gesture of love that you offer the Lord is answered with a lavish outpouring of His love in return. He can never be outdone in generosity.

PRAYER. *Jesus, help me dispel the emotional pain of sadness. I desire to give myself to You in a spirit of joy and thanksgiving. Thank You for assuring me that one day my heart will be full of joy.*

AND when you stand in prayer, forgive whatever you have against anybody. —Mt 5:24

JAN. 25

REFLECTION. In her book, *Something More*, Catherine Marshall writes about a time when she and her husband had problems that seemed to resist their prayers; they decided to act literally on Jesus' words, "And when you stand in prayer, forgive everyone."

So each day they spent time putting on paper any grievances they had against anybody. They read them aloud, forgave the persons involved, then destroyed the paper.

PRAYER. *Dear Jesus, help me to replace my emotional baggage with a forgiving heart. I will feel so much lighter.*

LOVE is never obnoxious. . . . —1 Cor 13:5a

JAN. 26

REFLECTION. Human judgment is so often clouded by feelings. We judge other people, and even ourselves, not so much on the objective evidence, but on feelings.

Put aside those bad feelings. Just laugh at them. Love your neighbor no matter how badly you might feel.

PRAYER. *Lord, help me to be polite when I feel like being rude.*

N O one lights a lamp to hide it in a corner . . . ; he places it on a stand so that all may see. —Lk 11:33

JAN.
27

REFLECTION. Holiness reveals itself in the last analysis as the fullness of life. It is expressed in the form of boundless happiness. It is the reflection of the light of Christ and God.

PRAYER. *Immerse me in Your light, O Lord. Let me feel You in my body, mind, heart, and soul.*

———————

L OVE bears all things.
—1 Cor 13:6

JAN.
28

REFLECTION. When Thomas Edison invented the electric light bulb in 1879, there were many failures along the way. At one point, his assistant in a fit of frustration, urged him to give up. "We have gone through thousands of experiments," he said, "and they have all failed." Edison snapped back, "Failed, no. We have learned thousands of experiments that do not work. We're getting closer."

Perseverance is the way to success.

PRAYER. *Dear Lord, I know the joy and celebration that awaits those who persevere. Help me to endure all things and plod along with confidence in reaching my goals.*

HIS is indeed a grace, if you endure the pain of unjust suffering because you are conscious of God.

—1 Pet 2:19

JAN.
29

REFLECTION. It is normal to want to run away from the cross. Do not be surprised if you are not up to carrying it. But how pleased the Lord is with those who pray for the grace to grin and bear it!

Even if they cry, their time of suffering can win rich rewards for themselves and for those they love.

PRAYER. *Help me, Lord, to be brave when I feel like caving in. I am very conscious of Your presence in my life.*

 ND I will ask the Father, and He will give you another Comforter to be with you forever, the Spirit of Truth . . . [Who] dwells with you.

—Jn 14:16-17

JAN.
30

REFLECTION. The Indwelling Trinity is closer to you than your own heartbeat. His comfort is available at will. Let the Lord be your strength, and your joy.

Like water at the kitchen sink, you need only turn on the spigot to draw it out; so is the Holy Spirit waiting to be invited into your life.

PRAYER. *Almighty God, I open myself to You; comfort me so that I may comfort others.*

UCH is the complete reliance upon God that we have through Christ. Obviously, we are not competent of ourselves to take credit for anything as coming from us. Our competence comes from God.

JAN.
31

—2 Cor 3:4-5

REFLECTION. The gift of confidence is deeper in your soul than you may imagine.

The mere fact that you are reading these daily meditations means that you are finding your confidence in Jesus. To pray to Christ is both to love Him and to rely on Him.

PRAYER. *Dear Jesus, I am hopeful, I am grateful, and I am confident thanks to You.*

HAVE come to understand that the sufferings of this present time are not worthy to be compared to the glory that is yet to come.

FEB.
1

—Rom 8:18

REFLECTION. True love involves pain. In order to give birth, a mother has to suffer, but glory follows pain.

Death is not extinguishing the light, it is putting out the lamp because the dawn has come. —*Rabindranath Tagore*

PRAYER. *Lord, when my time comes help me to accept it peacefully. Be my escort into heaven so that I will not be afraid.*

HEN the days for their purification were completed according to the Law of Moses, they brought the Child up to Jerusalem to present Him to the Lord. —Lk 2:22

FEB. 2

REFLECTION. Mary lifted up the Child Jesus when she presented Him at the Temple.

On this feast of the Presentation we offer ourselves along with Him to the glory of the Father.

PRAYER. *O Lord, help me to always remember that my faith is not simply a set of agreed upon beliefs. It is a truth that cuts to the marrow of my bones, a truth that must be lived every moment of my life. I offer myself to You body and soul.*

 ECEIVE the Holy Spirit; whose sins you shall forgive, they are forgiven. —Jn 20:22-23

FEB. 3

REFLECTION. On the feast of St. Blase, we have our throats blessed. The Holy Spirit cleanses us of every evil, in particular from diseases of the throat.

In this purgation we offer all our sins that they may be washed away forever.

PRAYER. *Lord Jesus, I bow before You in a spirit of thanksgiving. I have been made clean so many times in my life. Because of You I can now hold my head up high.*

THE Lord will give you rest, and you shall be like a watered garden. —Isa 58:11

FEB. 4

REFLECTION. Genuine happiness in the home is based on love that gives itself and sacrifices itself, simply and perseveringly.

This love can be sustained only with the food of faith, and faith is a gift of God that is nourished in prayer and the Sacraments.

—*Pope John Paul II*

PRAYER. *Holy Spirit of Love and Joy, thank You for filling me with Your wonderful life. The gift of Your love makes me happy to be alive. Help me to share my joy with everyone.*

SING praise to the Lord with the harp, with the harp and melodious song. With trumpets and the sound of horns sing joyfully. —Ps 98:5-6

FEB. 5

REFLECTION. As a manifestation of the human spirit, music performs a function that is noble, unique, and irreplaceable.

When music is truly beautiful and inspired, it speaks to us more than all the other acts of goodness, virtue, and peace.

—*Pope John Paul II*

PRAYER. *Dear Lord, thank You for my love of music. It rejoices my heart. I sing forever to Your glory.*

24

YOU shall love the Lord, your God, with your whole heart, and with your whole soul, and with all your strength. —Deut 6:5

FEB. 6

REFLECTION. It is possible to love God with your whole heart, mind, and soul, without forcing yourself to feel any emotion whatsoever. Simply will it. Will to love God, without making yourself feel anything.

The will has only one function, to say yes or no. If you want to love God, just say yes. Forget the feelings. The Lord is pleased with your holy desire, and He blesses you.

PRAYER. *Jesus, I will it. I will to love You. Help me to reach perfection one day, but for now, just be pleased that I give You myself as best I can.*

THE life that I live now in the flesh, I live in the faith of the Son of God. He loved me and gave Himself up for me. —Gal 2:20

FEB. 7

REFLECTION. The Eucharist is the privileged summit of the meeting of Christ's love for us; a love that is made available for each of us, a love that is made to be sacrificial lamb and food for our hunger for life.

As the Apostle says, "He loved me and gave Himself up for me." —*Pope Paul VI*

PRAYER. *Dear Jesus, in Your love I find my strength and joy.*

HE Lord has . . . sent me to bring Good News to the lowly, to bind up the brokenhearted, and to proclaim freedom for the captives. —Isa 61:1

FEB. 8

REFLECTION. This is the quote Jesus used in the synagogue to explain His mission.

We are members of Christ's Mystical Body, and so His mission is our mission too. Be glad, to spread His joy to others, to heal the sorrowful, and to liberate those caught up in the prison of self.

PRAYER. *O Lord, thank You for calling me to serve in the immense task of proclaiming the Good News of the Gospels.*

 ORD, You are at my side. —Ps 23:4

FEB. 9

REFLECTION. To love others is to be there for them. You share the joys and sorrows of those you love.

In the same way, the Lord is always at your side, sharing in your joys and sorrows. Believe in His love.

PRAYER. *Lord Jesus, I believe that Your love is stronger than death. Your life is more powerful than all the forces of nature combined. Let me be more aware that You are always at my side, giving me comfort and strength.*

26

AY your father and your mother have joy. May she who bore you be glad. —Prov 23:25

FEB. 10

REFLECTION. Give your parents a nice blessing today by resolving to live joyfully because of the knowledge of God's love.

They are happy when you are happy, and so is God.

PRAYER. *O Lord, Your love is at the center of my being. You are with my parents in the same way. Tell them I love them and give me the grace to live joyfully in Your Presence.*

 OVE . . . does not seek its own advantage. . . . —1 Cor 13:5b

FEB. 11

REFLECTION. Teach your heart to swim in the ocean of love. Do not take yourself too seriously.

Live in a state of awareness. Know that your smile can bring peace and joy to others.

PRAYER. *Lord, I need Your help in this. I want always to do Your Will. I never realized that Your Will includes my happiness here and now. I surrender to You, and ask You to teach me how to love and be joyful.*

27

HE Lord . . . answered me and delivered me from all my fear.

—Ps 34:4

FEB. 12

REFLECTION. A Bible that Abraham Lincoln often used as President falls open easily to Psalm 34. There is a smudge at one spot where the President apparently rested his fingers and meditated.

The verse is: "I sought the Lord, and He answered me and delivered me from all my fear."

PRAYER. *Calm my fears, O Lord, and relieve my anxiety. Let me place all my hopes in You. And when the storms threaten, assure me that You will guide me safely home.*

 OU have not chosen Me, but I have chosen you and have appointed you that you should bear fruit.

—Jn 15:16

FEB. 13

REFLECTION. It is through a loving knowledge of God that the soul, under the influence of wisdom, is prompted to judge all things in their relationship to God.

Wisdom elevates the soul above reason, above common sense, to a sympathy for the Divine point of view. It often conflicts with so-called "realistic thinking," or logic. God's ways are not man's.

PRAYER. *Dear Holy Spirit, You have chosen me and You lead me in directions I would not have chosen for myself. Give me the wisdom to discern Your Will and the courage to follow it.*

LOVE bears all things, believes all things, hopes all things, endures all things.

FEB. 14

—1 Cor 13:7

REFLECTION. Someone would have a poor idea of human and marital love by thinking that affection and joy vanish when difficulties come. This is when we really see what motivates people.

Here also is where gift and tenderness are consolidated, because true love does not think about itself, but about how to increase the good of the beloved. —Pope John Paul II

PRAYER. *Lord God, transform me into the compassionate, tender person I want to be. I give You my weakness in exchange for Your strength.*

OUR present light afflictions, which are for the moment, are achieving for us an eternal glory that is beyond all measure.

FEB. 15

—2 Cor 4:17

REFLECTION. The secret to sanctity and happiness rests in our fidelity to the duty of the present moment. —Jean Pierre de Caussaude

The will to bear discomfort in fulfilling that duty is the very basis of good character.

PRAYER. *Dear Jesus, help me to stay focused on the present moment, as I offer You all my joys and sufferings.*

F your eye is pure there will be sunshine in your soul.

—Mt 6:22

REFLECTION. Basically this means that if you have your eye set on the prize, the Kingdom of God, all the rest will pale by comparison. You will change and become light-hearted.

You will be free from the world of competition and greed. "Sunshine in your soul" means that you are living joyfully.

PRAYER. *Lord, help me to be pure of heart that I might live without fear and needless anxiety.*

————————

 HO is weak, and I do not feel weak? Who is led into sin, and I am not indignant? —2 Cor 11:29

REFLECTION. A Saint is someone who is weak enough to depend on God's strength.

A Saint is cheerful when it is difficult to be cheerful, and patient when most people would be ready to explode. A Saint pushes ahead when everyone says it is time to quit.

PRAYER. *Dear Lord, give me the weakness I need to turn to You automatically for strength. With You and in You I know all will be well.*

OVE is patient. . . .

—1 Cor 13:4

FEB.
18

REFLECTION. John Milton, in his sonnet on blindness, once wrote: "They also serve who only stand and wait." The service of love can often take the form of waiting.

God waits. The world He made is filled with waiting. Waiting is one of the primary laws of nature. Winter waits for spring. Buds wait for warmth. The earth waits for rain. Nothing in life comes to instant maturity.

PRAYER. *Jesus, my Lord, help me to realize that You will be with me in my times of waiting. Give me the patience of a Saint. that I may serve You faithfully.*

ET your main focus be on His Kingdom and HIs righteousness, and all these things will be given to you as well.

—Mt 6:33

FEB.
19

REFLECTION. By seeking God and His Holy Will above all things you become liberated from the acquisitive spirit.

God frees you from yourself, and nothing tastes sweeter than freedom.

PRAYER. *Jesus, my Lord, let me taste the freedom that You offer to those who love You. Let me grow in Your Spirit day by day, seeking You above all.*

EHOLD, I am the Lord, the God of all . . .
is there anything too hard for Me?
—Jer 32:27

**FEB.
20**

REFLECTION. Having confidence in the Lord is
the sign of true faith. It enables one to cross
over the threshold to the virtue of hope.

Hope in turn leads to the most delicious of
virtues, the virtue of trust. Once you trust the
Lord, your confidence is well established.

PRAYER. *Dear Lord, nothing is too difficult for
You. If only I could live in that knowledge on
a day to day basis. You will bring good out of
evil. In You all will be well.*

———————

HAT you believe will be done
for you.
—Mt 8:13

**FEB.
21**

REFLECTION. The words of Jesus are powerful
sources of encouragement. His choicest words
can make a huge difference in your life if you
put them into practice.

Try to trust Him and believe every word, for
what you believe will be done for you.

PRAYER. *O Lord, I want to live in Your love,
and allow You to use me as Your instrument.
Give me that special inspiration to believe
with an unshakable faith. Fill my lungs and
heart with songs of joy.*

A S the Father has loved Me, so have I loved you. Remain in My love.

—Jn 15:9

FEB. 22

REFLECTION. The Heart of Christ still beats. It unites millions of other hearts.

The Church sees the beauty of these hearts, which will surely proclaim a spiritual revival in our modern world. —*Pope Paul VI*

PRAYER. *Dear Sacred Heart of Jesus, make my heart like unto Yours. You are the vine, I am one branch among many. Keep me healthy in Your life, O Lord. Feed me Your energy and Your strength.*

T HE foolishness of God is wiser than human wisdom, and the weakness of God is stronger than human strength.

—1 Cor 1:25

FEB. 23

REFLECTION. Wisdom is able to distinguish between what is valuable and what is passing. The truly wise person will see the pearl of great price, which is heaven, and sell everything to possess it.

Wisdom is God speaking to us, calling us to nobility and glory. Pray for the gift of wisdom.

PRAYER. *O God of Light and Truth, give me wisdom that I may seek first Your Kingdom.*

O servants are greater than their master. If they have persecuted Me, they will persecute you also.

FEB. 24

—Jn 15:20

REFLECTION. There is no joy in this announcement. Who wants to be persecuted, or rejected?

Wisdom gives this answer: "Let your main focus be on His Kingdom, and these other things will be given to you" (Lk 12:31).

PRAYER. *O Lord, when I suffer the price of being Christian, especially at work, at school, or even in my family, remind me that You will never abandon those who suffer in Your Name.*

 E said to them, "Why are you fearful? Are you still without faith?"

FEB. 25

—Mk 4:40

REFLECTION. The evil one stirs up our fears to keep us suspicious, self-centered, immobile, and full of self-pity. In this way, Satan tries to put us in hell day by day.

But we are made for heaven. There is always grace to help us get to where God wants us to be. Grace is the communication of God's love, Jesus is the Mediator of Divine grace. He saves us from our fear.

PRAYER. *Help me, Lord, to banish fear. Enable me to understand that You are my strength and joy.*

SK, and it will be given to you; seek, and you will find; knock, and the door will be opened to you. For everyone who asks will receive, and those who seek will find, and to those who knock the door will be opened.

FEB. 26

—Mt 7:7-8

REFLECTION. Trust comes with difficulty. When our feet are buried in quicksand, fear envelops us. We are tempted in times of turmoil to reach for alcohol or drugs, anything to soothe that savage feeling of fear.

This is the time to cry out to Jesus for help.

PRAYER. *Quiet my troubled soul, O Lord, and give me Your hand to lift me up. Lead me to safety, and I will follow You.*

 AY the peace of God, which surpasses all understanding, guard your hearts and your minds in Christ Jesus.

FEB. 27

—Phil 4:7

REFLECTION. The older we get, the greater becomes our inclination to give thanks, especially heavenward. We feel more strongly than we could possibly have ever felt before that life is a free gift . . . and every hour . . . an unexpected gift to be gratefully received.

—Martin Buber

PRAYER. *Dear Father, how fortunate I am to enjoy the gift of life. Thank You.*

JUST as a father has compassion on his children, the Lord has compassion on those who fear Him. —Ps 103:13

FEB. 28

REFLECTION. All my life I have noticed that outstanding people of every religion have something very special in common.

They all possess the fundamental wisdom that we are children of a gracious God, a God Who loves us dearly, and they are grateful. Their gratitude gives them sweetness of spirit.

PRAYER. *Grant me, O Lord, sweetness of spirit, which is born of reverential fear. I feel Your compassion, and it makes me happy.*

DO not be frightened. But set apart Christ as Lord in your hearts. —1 Pet 3:14-15

FEB. 29

REFLECTION. Jesus is the center of the universe, and the center of your heart. In Him you live and breathe and have your being.

You can trust Him. When you give Him your life, He gives Himself right back to you in return.

PRAYER. *Be the center of my life, Lord Jesus. Be closer to me than my own heartbeat. Let our love be one, and our life be one, now and forever.*

T IS not the healthy who need a physician, but rather those who are sick. Go and learn what this text means: "I desire mercy, not sacrifice." I have come to call not the righteous but sinners. —Mt 9:12-13

MAR. 1

REFLECTION. This is the Good News of the Gospel. Jesus explicitly says that God will judge us on the degree of mercy we exhibit toward others, not on the number of times we offer ritual sacrifices.

Also, He says that His first concern is to save sinners.

PRAYER. *Dear Lord, I thank You for this revelation. I am a sinner in what I have done, and in what I have left undone. This assurance of Your mercy brings joy to my soul.*

 AY all who seek You rejoice in You and be jubilant. May those who love Your salvation cry out forever, "The Lord be magnified."—Ps 40:17

MAR. 2

REFLECTION. The word "joy" conjures up images of celebration, full-bodied laughter, or feelings of enchantment. But there is another dimension. Joy is essentially a share in God's inmost Being.

God is perfectly whole, needing nothing for completion. He possesses in Himself the fullness of Being and Life. Joy is God's life.

PRAYER. *Heavenly Father, thank You for Your promise of eternal joy. Please allow me the privilege of living joyfully right now.*

EEK no revenge and bear no grudge **MAR.**
against your fellow countrymen.
—Lev 19:18 **3**

REFLECTION. A spirit of forgiveness is the first step toward joy.

"Prophetic religion through the ages has stressed the need for forgiveness and tolerance . . . psychology now supplements this insight by teaching us that we can achieve inner health only through forgiveness—the forgiveness not only of others but also of ourselves."

—*Joshua Liebman*

PRAYER. *Dear Lord, I have forgiven others their faults, but I have a hard time forgiving myself for my own. Give me the spirit of forgiveness, for myself as well as others.*

 HE just man rejoices in the Lord and **MAR.**
seeks refuge in Him.
—Ps 64:11 **4**

REFLECTION. The great theologian and scientist Pierre Teilhard de Chardin saw God in every living thing.

Here is a beautiful prayer he wrote.

PRAYER. *I thank You, my God, for having in a thousand ways led my eyes to discover the immense simplicity of things. . . . I can no longer see anything, nor any longer breathe outside that milieu in which all is made one.*

E are God's coworkers.

—1 Cor 3:9

 MAR.
5

REFLECTION.

I am only one
but still I am one.
I cannot do everything
but still I can do something.
I will not refuse to do the something
that I can do. —*Edward Everett Hall*

PRAYER. *Dear Lord, help me to believe in myself. With You living in me, I can make a difference.*

 HY are you cast down, O my
soul? . . . praise Him, Who is the
health of my countenance and
my God. —Ps 42:11

MAR.
6

REFLECTION. The thoughts that you think are the direct cause of your emotional life. Like thunder follows lightning, so do feelings follow thoughts.

You cannot control your feelings by sheer will power, but you can control your thoughts. Think positively. With the help of your faith, your feelings will soon brighten up.

PRAYER. *Lord Jesus, so often when people are in pain, they feel as if they are abandoned or are being punished. Help me to see that feelings are not facts in these matters. Help me to be joyful.*

BEAR with one another, and forgive one another if anyone has reason to be offended. . . . You must forgive just as the Lord has forgiven you. —Col 3:13

REFLECTION. Ann Landers advised a woman who had a husband with a "wandering eye": "Don't be stubborn or proud. Take him back. I promise you won't regret it."

The woman felt unable to forgive, but she took the advice because it seemed meant for her. "The eight years that followed were the happiest," she wrote, noting that her husband had recently died. "The warmth of the memories of our last years together will stay with me forever."

PRAYER. *Give me the power to forgive, O Lord, as You have forgiven me.*

———————

IF we confess our sins, He is faithful and forgives our sins; He cleanses us from all unrighteousness. —1 Jn 1:9

REFLECTION. There are two stages of Christian forgiveness. The first is forgiveness itself, the second is thanksgiving. Nothing erases the hurts of the past faster than a grateful heart.

We have so much for which to be grateful. When we concentrate on the good things of life, our hurts become insignificant.

PRAYER. *How grateful I am, O Lord, for the gift of forgiveness. Even though I have sinned, I trust in Your mercy.*

ANYONE who wishes to follow Me must deny himself, take up his cross, and follow Me. —Mk 8:34

REFLECTION. Those who do not deny themselves suffer the consequences—as seen in this prose-poem from Alcoholics Anonymous.

We drank for happiness and became unhappy. / We drank for joy and became miserable. / We drank for sociability and became argumentative. / We drank for sophistication and became obnoxious. / We drank for friendship and made enemies. / We drank for sleep and awakened without rest.

PRAYER. *Dear Lord, teach me the truth that self-love is better than self-destruction.*

BE not afraid. —Mt 14:27

REFLECTION. There is a certain kind of fear that is called jealousy. Jealousy is an unpleasant feeling of suspicion arising from the fear or mistrust of another. Jealous people are always afraid of losing someone or something. They become irrational, bringing misery to all concerned.

Fear often seems to signal the presence of some external danger. But the real danger is from within—from our own jealousy.

PRAYER. *Lord, deliver me from jealousy so that my joy may be complete.*

ERVE the Lord with gladness; come into His presence with joy.

MAR.
11

—Ps 99:2

REFLECTION. Being an angel of peace, and a messenger of joy is the best kind of evangelization. Do you know why? Because the world loves a cheerful giver.

Let your light shine for all to see.

PRAYER. *Heavenly Father, make me an instrument of Your peace. Where there is hatred let me bring love . . . Where there is doubt, faith and where there is sadness, joy.*

AY we rejoice in your victory and in the Name of our God raise banners; may the Lord fulfill all your petitions.

MAR.
12

—Ps 20:6

REFLECTION. Avoid the "wagon-train" mentality where small groups close in on themselves to fight against the outside world. They often become their own worst enemies.

Pray for atheists, agnostics, and secular humanists. They are human beings whom God loves and wants to save. God became man to save the lost sheep.

PRAYER. *Father, give me spiritual vision, open my eyes to see and love all those whom You love, even the ones who reject You outright.*

YOU must treat the proselyte who resides with you like the native born among you. —Lev 19:34

MAR. 13

REFLECTION. Sometimes we have to make a little effort to accept foreigners. Jesus was accused of walking with sinners. He taught us not to look down our noses at those less fortunate than we.

Love even when you do not feel like loving.

PRAYER. *Dear Lord, help me to love as You love, without discrimination.*

FILL us with Your love that all our days we may sing for joy. —Ps 90:14

MAR. 14

REFLECTION. The greatest honor you can give to Almighty God, greater than all your sacrifices and mortifications, is to live gladly, joyfully because of the knowledge of His love.

—*Bl. Juliana of Norwich*

To be filled with God is to be filled with God's infinite joy. His love is His joy.

PRAYER. *Heavenly Father, I am beginning to realize the fact that to come closer to You is to come closer to Joy itself. You are the fullness of happiness. You pine for nothing. Thank You for drawing me closer to You, my strength and my joy.*

43

LOVE one another with mutual affection, anticipating one another with honor.

—Rom 12:10

MAR.

15

REFLECTION. We ought to be as cheerful as we can, if only because to be happy ourselves is a most effectual contribution to the happiness of others. —*John Lubbok, 1890*

Love and joy and cheer are inseparable companions.

PRAYER. *Jesus, my Lord and my God, let Your love live in me that I may beam with the happiness that only You can give.*

OTHER seeds fell on rich soil and produced an abundant crop. . . . Listen, anyone who has ears to hear.

—Mt 13:8

MAR.

16

REFLECTION. The seeds of the parable represent the Word of God. When the Word of God falls on good soil it grows and produces a rich harvest.

You become the good soil when you listen. Practice the art of spiritual listening. Read slowly and absorb the wisdom.

PRAYER. *Holy Spirit, I do listen to Your Word. Give me the deeper wisdom that comes from loving You. Help me to produce abundant good fruit.*

MAY you continue to seek perfection and be completely accepting of the Will of God. —Col 4:12

MAR.
17

REFLECTION. When St. Patrick was asked to return to Ireland, the land where he was once in prison, he recoiled at the idea.

Nevertheless, he mustered the courage to obey, and became the greatest missionary in Irish history.

PRAYER. *Father, there comes a time when obeying Your Will is the only thing to do if we want interior peace. Let me know Your Will in my life so that I may learn to follow Your plan and not my own.*

ALL who take refuge in You will be happy and forever shout for joy. —Ps 5:12

MAR.
18

REFLECTION. Even secular writers agree that joy is a sign of great wisdom. Here are a few examples:

The plainest sign of wisdom is a continual cheerfulness. —*Michel de Montaigne, 1580*

A light heart lives long. —*William Shakespeare, 1595*

Cheerfulness keeps up a kind of daylight in the mind. —*Joseph Addison, 1712*

PRAYER. *Holy Spirit, I take refuge in You. Now fill me with Your heavenly peace and joy.*

IVE joy to the soul of Your servant, for to You I lift up my soul.

—Ps 86:4

MAR.
19

REFLECTION. St. Joseph was a man of peace and joy. He was also a grateful man. How important it is for us to be grateful in all circumstances.

The variety of gifts we all possess in common gives balance to the Church; therefore, we can rejoice in the gifts God gives to others.

PRAYER. *Father of us all, let my soul rejoice in Your love. Give me the grace to imitate the virtue of good St. Joseph. Help me to be humble and strong.*

OME to Me, all you who labor and are burdened, and I will refresh you.

—Mt 11:28

MAR.
20

REFLECTION. It is in the *now* of time that we discover God. Listening in silence leads to happiness because it leads toward God.

The degree to which we focus on yesterday or tomorrow is the degree to which we miss the holiness of the present moment.

PRAYER. *Dear Lord, You are the soul of my soul. Teach me to come to You immediately when I am in distress. Help me to see that You, living in me, will be my refreshment and light.*

E of good cheer.

REFLECTION. No matter who you are, or what your circumstance in life, it is possible to be brave and cheerful.

"God has created me to do Him some definite service; He has committed some work to me which He has not committed to another. . . .

"Therefore I will trust Him. If I am in sickness, my sickness may serve Him; in perplexity, my perplexity may serve Him; if I am in sorrow, my sorrow may serve Him."

—*Cardinal Newman*

PRAYER. *Dear Lord, I am at Your service with a smile. Help me to act bravely in spite of my fears.*

F you do good to those who do good to you, what credit is that to you? Even sinners do as much.

REFLECTION. Nearly all great human achievements begin with the inspiration and hard work of one dedicated person.

When individuals are responsible, society prospers; when they lose their sense of responsibility, society decays.

PRAYER. *Help me, Lord, to be a living instrument of Your love. Show me the way.*

ROW in the grace and knowledge of **MAR.** our Lord and Savior, Jesus Christ.
—2 Pet 3:18 **23**

REFLECTION. Those who fall into the trap of believing that institutions are too big to change forget the lessons of history. Institutions are changed all the time by reform movements from within.

You can change the world if you put your mind to it. Join in common cause with others who share your passion. Be a reformer as Jesus was.

PRAYER. *Jesus, You are my rock and my strength. Help me to gain deeper insight into the truth that I can do all things through You Who strengthen me.*

 CAME not to condemn the world but to **MAR.** save it.
—Jn 12:47 **24**

REFLECTION. We are all saved by the Blood of Christ. He died for everyone, including the least among us. We in turn must learn to die a little for others day by day.

There are 86,400 seconds in a day. How many seconds do you devote to yourself? How many are devoted to helping your neighbor?

PRAYER. *Jesus, I accept Your challenge and Your saving love. I will try to share the gifts and the joy You have given me, especially with those less fortunate than I.*

ET the little children come to Me. . . . **MAR.**
For it is to such as these that the Kingdom of God belongs.
25
—Mk 10:14

REFLECTION. Early on, Mother Teresa of Calcutta told her sisters that Jesus comes into
this world in many distressing disguises. For
instance, whenever they met persons with the
smell of death on them, they were to treat
such persons as they would Jesus Christ.

The sisters listened because they truly had
the childlike spirit, and they reaped a rich spiritual harvest.

PRAYER. *Dear Lord, help me to see You living
in all Your children wherever they may be. I
want to have the faith of a little child that I
may serve You well in this life and the next.*

LL will know that you are My disci- **MAR.**
ples, if you love one another.
—Jn 13:35
26

REFLECTION. We need more doers, fewer talk-
ers: more to say it can be done, fewer who
give up trying, more to inspire others with
confidence, fewer who throw cold water on
anyone taking a positive initiative.

—James Keller, founder of The Christophers

PRAYER. *Father, make me sparkle with opti-
mism. Teach me how to be a positive, constructive force in this world.*

FOR this I came into the world, to bear witness to the truth. Everyone who is of the truth hears My voice. —Jn 18:37

REFLECTION. Each person's mission is a mission of love.

Begin in the place where you are, with the people closest to you. Make your homes centers of compassion and forgive endlessly. Let no one ever come to you without coming away better and happier. —*Mother Teresa*

PRAYER. *Dear Jesus, I know that charity begins at home. Let me begin there. Teach me how to bring a little more happiness to those closest to me. From there, I will branch out to everyone I meet.*

HUSBANDS, love your wives just as Christ loved the Church. —Eph 5:25

REFLECTION. Ultimately success in communicating love is a matter of openness to God's Spirit. Those who love best learn how to make God's strength and joy their own. Take care of first things first.

Believing in God's love is the greatest stimulant to human love.

PRAYER. *Holy Spirit, You are the Lover within Who teaches us the art of loving. Teach me how to be sensitive and kind.*

OU shall love the Lord your God with all your heart, and with all your soul, and with all your mind. This is the greatest and the first commandment. The second is like it: "You shall love your neighbor as yourself." —Mt 22:37-40

MAR. 29

REFLECTION. Christian ascetism, when properly lived, renders a person more open to a life of loving service.

The more you get outside of yourself, the freer you become to be happy.

PRAYER. *Heavenly Father, teach me how to love. Teach me to render others more cheerful by my cheerfulness. Since service focuses on the good of the neighbor, empower me to forget myself as I strive to do good.*

F you keep My commandments, you will remain in My love, just as I have kept My Father's commandments and remain in His love. —Jn 15:10

MAR. 30

REFLECTION. Those who obey the Lord become free of the tyranny of self-reproach. They do not listen to that demon within which always puts them down, saying things like, "You're too fat," or, "You're stupid," or, "You're no good."

Make yourself more available to others and you will be freed from needless anxiety.

PRAYER. *Jesus, how I love Your wisdom. I thrill at the idea that You are living in me, and I am living in You..*

LESSED are the pure of heart, for they will see God. —Mt 5:8 **MAR.**
31

REFLECTION. Purity is the virtue that is most ridiculed. It is associated with impotence, narrowness of spirit and fear of life, while in fact it is the liberating power that opens the doors of true freedom, peace, and joy.

True purity of heart is found in unselfish love.

PRAYER. *Heavenly Father, make my heart like unto Yours. Give me the grace to see the world as Jesus saw it.*

I AM the Good Shepherd, and I know Mine and they know Me. —Jn 10:14 **APR.**
1

REFLECTION. The Lord is compared to a shepherd. He leads His flock and sees that His sheep have water and a good pasture on which to graze.

We have a good shepherd in our lives . . . what a joy it is to feel safe and sound.

PRAYER. *Dear Jesus, You are the Good Shepherd, and I am one of Your many sheep. You care for me and protect me. You come after me when I stray. Can I ever thank You enough?*

YOUR hands made me and shaped me; give me wisdom to learn Your commands. —Ps 119:73

REFLECTION. The Saints provide us with wonderful examples of heroic love. We experience the Lord's life flowing through them.

It makes one realize how God has fashioned each of us. We too are called to be instruments of His love.

PRAYER. *Dear Lord, make me an instrument of Your peace. Where there is sadness let me bring joy, and where there is hatred let me bring love.*

DO not be afraid. I bring you good tidings of great joy. —Lk 2:10

REFLECTION. As people, we are meant to have human joys: the joy of living, the joy of love and friendship, the joy of work well done.

As Christians, we have cause for further joy: like Jesus, we know that we are loved by God our Father. —*Pope John Paul II*

PRAYER. *Dearest Jesus, because of You I am no longer afraid. Well, let's say I am much less afraid. I thank You for this untrembling center You put in my soul.*

YOU love justice and hate wickedness. Therefore, God, your God, has anointed you with the oil of gladness.

—Ps 45:8

APR. 4

REFLECTION. Ludwig Feuerbach, sometimes called the father of the anti-God movement, wrote this in 1831: "The turning point in history will be the moment when man becomes aware that the only God of man is man himself. We have to replace the love of God with the love of man."

Adolph Hitler said Feuerbach was his favorite philosopher.

PRAYER. *Deliver me, O Lord, from all evil. Protect me from those who abuse others. Give me the grace to remain faithful to You.*

BEAR one another's burdens, and in this way you will fulfill the law of Christ.

—Gal 6:2

APR. 5

REFLECTION. "Charity begins at home," but it also reaches out to others. The whole family can cooperate in all kinds of love projects. It takes planning and time, but it can be done.

Perhaps something like a "family night" would be welcomed by everybody and provide some memorable experiences.

PRAYER. *Dear Lord, open my eyes so that I may be more sensitive, more caring and more helpful to my family members.*

54

LESSED are the poor in spirit, for theirs is the Kingdom of Heaven. **APR. 6**

—Mt 5:3

REFLECTION. In His Sermon on the Mount (Mt 5:1-10) Jesus taught these values:

Be meek and humble.
Be a comfort to others.
Be merciful.
Be clean of heart.
Be a peacemaker.
Be willing to suffer for justice's sake.

PRAYER. *O Lord, my pride and laziness often blind me to my higher calling. Give me the clarity and strength to be poor in spirit.*

ET them give thanks to the Lord for His kindness and for the wonders He does for people. He has satisfied the thirsty and filled the hungry. **APR. 7**

—Ps 107:8-9

REFLECTION. The prayer of thanksgiving is itself the prelude to the prayer of praise. When we pause in quiet praise of God, the need for words diminishes and we enter an atmosphere of joyful silence.

This quiet time is restful and full of peace. It is called the gift of contemplation, and it flourishes in a grateful heart.

PRAYER. *Father, humbly I bow before You, and bathe in the warmth of Your love.*

E compel every thought to surrender in obedience to Christ.
—2 Cor 10:5

APR.
8

REFLECTION. No heaven can come to us unless our hearts find rest in today. Take heaven.

No peace lies in the future that is not hidden in the present moment. Take peace.

The gloom of the world is but a shadow. Behind it, yet within our reach, is joy. Take joy.

PRAYER. *Dear Lord, help me to take responsibility for my thoughts. Help me to banish every drop of self-pity.*

EAR the Lord, you holy ones; nothing is lacking for those who fear Him. —Ps 34:10

APR.
9

REFLECTION. The Lord God knows all things. He knows what you really need, not merely what you think you need.

Trust Him to take care of you in His own way. Life may hurt from time to time, but He knows what He is doing.

PRAYER. *Lord, I turn over my needs and my very self to You. I never seem to do it completely so I am not sure if You think I am sincere or not. But I want to be. I give myself to You warts and all, and I know that You will receive me kindly.*

FAITH then depends on hearing, and hearing on the Word of Christ. . . . "Their voice has gone forth into all the earth."

APR. 10

—Rom 10:17-18

REFLECTION. Apparently, not everyone hears the message. In 1888 Friedrich Nietzsche wrote: "God is dead. It is we who have killed him. . . . We are the assassins of God. . . . We are at war against the Christian ideal, against the doctrine that makes beatitudes and salvation the aim of life."

Hitler idolized Nietzsche, and we know the evil that flowed from his life.

PRAYER. *Dear Jesus, an evil root produces evil fruit. Cleanse me of all evil, and bring me into the realm of Your joy.*

GOD created human beings in His image, in the image of God He created them, male and female He created them.

APR. 11

—Gen 1:27

REFLECTION. Atheistic humanism was bound to end in bankruptcy—if man takes himself as a God, he can for a time cherish the illusion that he freed himself, but it is a fleeting exultation.

In reality, he has merely abased God, and it is not long before he abases himself.

PRAYER. *Father of Life and Love, deliver me from the father of lies, and from the spirit of atheism, that I may prosper in the joy of loving You.*

WE no person anything except to
love one another; for whoever loves
his neighbor has fulfilled the Law.

—Rom 13:8

APR.
12

REFLECTION. Jesus said, "This is My commandment, that you love one another as I have loved you" (Jn 15:12). He said this on the night before He died.

That people should love one another was not new. The command was contained in the Hebrew bible, but Jesus extended it to include one's enemies.

PRAYER. *Dear Lord, in my heart of hearts I pray for the grace to love as You loved.*

THOUGH the mountains may depart
and the hills may waver, My kindness
shall not depart from you.

—Isa 54:10

APR.
13

REFLECTION. God is unchanging love. His kindness endures forever. Everything in existence belongs to Him.

Begin now to love Him with your whole heart. Believe in His eternal kindness.

PRAYER. *Heavenly Father, I am certain that You give Yourself to me wholeheartedly. In return, I want to give myself to You heart and soul.*

HAT shall I render to the Lord for all He has given me? I will take the chalice of salvation and call upon the Name of the Lord.

APR. 14

—Ps 116:12-13

REFLECTION. Why not give the Lord a loving heart?

St. Peter, quoting the Book of Proverbs, says, "Love covers a multitude of sins" (1 Pet 4:8). Love conquers all.

Sinful persons reject God's love and say: "I'll do it my way!" But if they repent and turn their lives around, they win His favor.

PRAYER. *Lord, at Mass each day I unite spiritually with Jesus as He offers Himself to the Father.*

 O not be concerned about your life and what you will have to eat or drink, or about your body and what you will wear. Surely life is more than food, and the body is more than clothing.

APR. 15

—Mt 6:25

REFLECTION. Joy is the sign of the Holy Spirit's presence because a joyful person obeys the Lord.

Putting aside needless worry is possible. Otherwise Jesus would not have told you to stop worrying.

PRAYER. *Dear Lord, I hear Your counsel; now all I need to do is make the decision to will it into reality. I will not worry about petty things. I will entrust them to You and let You worry about them for me.*

GLAD heart makes a cheerful face, but by grief of mind the spirit is cast down. —Prov 15:13

APR. 16

REFLECTION. A grain of sand finds its way inside the shell of an oyster. The intruder, though microscopic, is a source of irritation and pain to the soft body of the oyster. Unable to rid itself of the unwelcome pebble, the oyster seeks to reduce the irritation by coating it with layers of soft, iridescent mother-of-pearl material from its own shell.

Over time, the oyster transforms a painful irritation into a beautiful pearl of great value.

PRAYER. *Dear Lord, please help me to make spiritual pearls of joy out of the grains of sorrow in my life.*

ESUS took the loaves, and when He had given thanks, He distributed them to the people who were sitting there. He did the same with the fish, distributing to them as much as they wanted. —Jn 6:11

APR. 17

REFLECTION. The feeling of hunger is the body's way of urging us to take nourishment. The feeling of longing and emptiness is the soul's way of reminding us that we hunger for God.

St. Augustine said, "Our hearts will remain restless until they rest in You, O Lord."

PRAYER. *Dear Jesus, when I receive You in the Eucharist I know You nourish my soul with the gift of peace and joy. Help me to abide in You.*

THERE are three things in which I delight, and they are beautiful in the sight of the Lord and of human beings: concord among brothers and sisters, friendship among neighbors, and husband and wife who live in perfect harmony. —Sir 25:1

REFLECTION. It is characteristic that you want to know more, but you do not live up to what you already know. If you want to make God happy, then be a good neighbor to one and all. Practice the Golden Rule.

PRAYER. *Lord, send us as witnesses of the Gospel into a world of fragile peace and broken promises. We ask this through Christ our Lord.*

 WHICH of you loves life and desires to see good days? Keep your tongue from evil. —Ps 34:13-14

REFLECTION. If you want to live in peace, make sure that you do not make enemies by poisoning the atmosphere with vicious gossip. If you want to live joyfully, control your speech and avoid negativity.

PRAYER. *Help me, Lord, to control my tongue so that I may say only what is good and charitable. Make me an instrument of Your peace.*

ALL flesh is like grass, and all its glory like the flower of the field. The grass withers, and the flower fades, but the word of the Lord endures forever.

APR. **20**

—1 Pet 1:24-25

REFLECTION. If you want to be happy, if you want to be calm and peaceful, if you want your life to be filled with joy: pray.

Peace, joy, and happiness are the fruits of silent prayer.

PRAYER. *Lord, our God, fill us with Your Spirit so that we may hear Your Good News. Touch our hearts with Your love so that we in turn may love one another.*

———

FOR I determined not to know anything among you, except Jesus Christ and Him crucified. —1 Cor 2:2

APR. **21**

REFLECTION. Jesus taught us that in spite of pain, we were made for joy. It may be your lot one day to pass through the agony of a Good Friday before reaching the joy of an Easter Sunday. But do not be afraid.

If you cling to God, He will see you safely through the storm.

PRAYER. *Lord, help me to understand the astounding love that You expressed on the Cross, and enable me to respond to that love with all my heart.*

HE God of all consolation . . . consoles us in all our afflictions and thereby enables us to console others in their troubles. —2 Cor 1:3-4

REFLECTION. Suffering is a tremendous mystery for all of us. Jesus taught us how to give meaning to suffering by embracing the Cross. He accepted the Cross as His special vocation.

He did not want it, no one in his right mind would want pain, but He used it as a coin to purchase our salvation.

PRAYER. *Dear Jesus, comfort me, console me, and inspire me so that I may comfort and console and inspire those who need me.*

 Y Father, if this cup cannot pass away unless I drink it, Your Will be done. —Mt 26:42

REFLECTION. These words were given in a private revelation to Bl. Henry Suso (1327):

"Suffering converts a worldly person into a heavenly person. Suffering makes one a stranger to the world and gives him My continual intimacy. It decreases friends and increases grace."

PRAYER. *Father, I am repelled by the cross. Help me to say the words Jesus said the night before He died: If possible remove this cross from me, but not my will but Yours be done.*

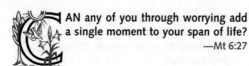

AN any of you through worrying add a single moment to your span of life?
—Mt 6:27

REFLECTION. Think about it. You are killing yourself with petty anxieties. You can control your thoughts. Trusting thoughts will bring you peace of mind.

Why are you doing this? Jesus is asking you point blank. Why are you afraid?

PRAYER. *Jesus, my Lord, I really do not know what I am doing half the time. Give me the grace to be strong enough to put a halt to this way of life. I deserve a better life, and with Your help, I am going to claim it.*

———————————

OME away with Me, by yourselves, to a deserted place and rest for a while.
—Mk 6:31

REFLECTION. On this feast day of St. Mark, we pause to look into the face and the eyes of Jesus.

Close the door of the soul to all the noise of the outside world, and there, alone with God, pray slowly the words Jesus taught us.

PRAYER. *Our Father Who art in heaven, hallowed be Thy Name; Thy Kingdom come; . . .*

THE two disciples described what had happened on their journey and how He had made Himself known to them in the breaking of the bread. —Lk 24:35

APR. 26

REFLECTION. Each day at Holy Mass Catholics kneel in the Presence of the Blessed Eucharist.

They recognize the Lord's true Presence and worship Him in a spirit of joy, as they receive Holy Communion.

PRAYER. *How blessed and privileged we are, O Lord, to recognize You in the breaking of the Holy Bread, and to be nourished by You.*

THIS is the day that the Lord has made; let us exult and rejoice in it. —Ps 118:24

APR. 27

REFLECTION. Wherever there is a heart that overcomes selfishness, violence, and hatred—wherever there is a heart that reaches out to someone in need—Christ is risen from the dead, risen today. . . .

May the whole world rise in Him. Alleluia.

—Pope John Paul II

PRAYER. *Father, Son, and Holy Spirit, we rejoice in Your joy and we live in Your love. Help me to reach out to someone in need today.*

THEY were amazed to see the fearlessness shown by Peter and John and to discover that they were uneducated ordinary men. —Acts 4:13

APR. 28

REFLECTION. Joy and confidence are true signs of the presence of the Holy Spirit. It was the Spirit Who raised Jesus from the dead, and the same Spirit lifts us all above our weakness.

What an amazing cause for joy! We are not alone. The Lord lives in us.

PRAYER. *Holy Spirit, soul of my soul, live in me and give me the courage to proclaim the glory of Your Name.*

FOR the doctrine of the Cross is foolishness to those who are perishing, but to those who are saved, that is, to us, it is the power of God. —1 Cor 1:18

APR. 29

REFLECTION. Too many people would have you believe that the perfume of God is pain and suffering. It is not. Love comes in many disguises. The cross is a sign of total self-giving and love.

God's perfume is happiness.

PRAYER. *O Lord, grant me the courage to take up my cross and follow You. Make me understand that it is through the cross that I learn how to die with You, so that I may also rise with You.*

ESUS our Lord . . . was handed over to death for our sins and was raised for our justification. —Rom 4:24-25

REFLECTION. Jesus was afraid in the garden that night.

He was not afraid of death itself, but of the manner in which He would die. He was human like us.

When you are feeling afraid, remember that the servant cannot be greater than the master.

PRAYER. *Lord, teach me not to run away from my cross. By Your Holy Cross You have redeemed the world.*

HE Spirit helps us in our weakness. For we do not know how to pray as we should, but the Spirit Himself intercedes for us with sighs that cannot be put into words. —Rom 8:26

REFLECTION. There are many kinds of prayer: liturgical, vocal, and contemplative prayer, to name a few.

However, there is one prayer that is unlearned and spontaneous. It is the prayer that comes from the Holy Spirit acting in the depths of the soul.

PRAYER. *Dear Jesus, open the eyes of my heart that I may see You and enjoy Your smile. Even when I am exhausted and full of pain, Your Spirit prays in me and through me.*

THEREFORE, I say to you: ask, and it will be given you.

—Lk 11:9

REFLECTION. We often pray by our gut feelings. A confused teenager may find himself crying out, "God, I don't know where I'm going, I don't know what I want, or what I should do. Help me."

Or a young mother will catch herself saying, "Please, God, help me get through this day without murdering my children." These are cries of pain that are real prayers.

PRAYER. *Lord, how many times I have cried to You for help. Thank You for being there whenever I needed You.*

HEN you pray, go into your room, close the door, and pray to your Father in secret.

—Mt 6:6

REFLECTION. God does not make Himself heard in any voice that reaches your ears, but in a voice that your heart can well perceive.

He will then speak to you by such interior lights, such sweet touches in your heart, such tokens of forgiveness . . . in a word, such voices of love, as are well understood by those souls whom He loves and who seek for nothing but Himself alone. —*St. Alphonsus Liguori*

PRAYER. *Lord, I am here. I love You. Help me to be quiet and attentive.*

ESUS gave them this answer, "Amen, amen, I say to you, the Son can do nothing by Himself. He can do only what He sees the Father doing." —Jn 5:19

MAY 4

REFLECTION. Be patient with God. Wait for Him to lead you. To pray means to ascend. We ascend to the source of our power, the source of our joy.

He will come to show you the way with clarity.

PRAYER. *Lord Jesus, teach me how to pray even as You taught Your disciples. Send Your Spirit into my heart so that I may pray with You to the Father, and follow His Will.*

E said to them in reply, "Why are you so frightened, O you of little faith?" —Mt 8:26

MAY 5

REFLECTION. God calls you by name. He sees you and understands you as He made you. He knows what is in you, all your peculiar feelings and thoughts, your dispositions and likings, your strength, and your weakness.

He views you in your day of rejoicing and in your day of sorrow. He sympathizes in your hopes and your temptations. . . . He hears your voice, the beating of your heart and your very breathing. —*Cardinal Newman*

PRAYER. *Almighty God in heaven, You know me, I belong to You.*

D O not be afraid. . . . Behold, your **MAY** King. —Jn 12:15 **6**

REFLECTION. To contemplate is simply to enjoy God. It is not an intellectual process. It is not thinking about God. You simply sense His loving Presence filling you, and you love Him in return.

Remember, your union with God depends more on His love for you, than on your love for Him. Contemplative prayer is being in love with God. To love God is to enjoy Him.

PRAYER. *Almighty Father, Holy One, Lord of Lords, I love You. Help me to love You more and more. Let me bathe in the splendor of Your warmth.*

A ND when I am lifted up from the **MAY** earth [on the Cross], I will draw everyone to Myself. —Jn 12:32 **7**

REFLECTION. In dying, Jesus thought of you. He gave His life that you might have eternal life. He draws all those whom you love to Himself. Your prayers for your loved ones are being answered.

Be glad and rejoice in His love.

PRAYER. *Thank You, Jesus, for lifting me up above my petty concerns.*

70

F your hand causes you to sin, cut it off. **MAY**

—Mk 9:42

8

REFLECTION. Does Christ expect you to mutilate yourself? Certainly not. Even the strictest fundamentalist would admit that we cannot take this passage literally.

We must, however, do everything in our power to attain the Kingdom.

PRAYER. *Father, once again I am painfully aware that I am not capable of saving myself. That is why I am so indebted to You, so grateful and joyful because of the knowledge of Your love.*

———————

 OD our Savior . . . desires everyone **MAY**
to be saved and to come to full
knowledge of the truth.

—1 Tim 2:4

9

REFLECTION. Perhaps this explains why you have received the cross you must carry. By your union with Jesus, you are sharing in the work of Redemption.

Maybe the soul of a loved one is being saved by your life.

PRAYER. *Lord, I am baffled by the mystery of suffering. Help me to do all in my power to lighten my burden, but in the end help me to surrender to my destiny. Your love for me is my greatest gift. Thank You.*

71

ELIGHT in the Lord, and He will give you what you desire.

—Ps 37:4

REFLECTION. Jesus speaks to you: "I know you want to live for My love, gladly suffering all the penance that might come to you. But inasmuch as you do not live without sin, you are depressed and sorrowful . . . yet do not be too much vexed with the sin that falls to you against your will. . . . I keep you most securely."

—Bl. Juliana of Norwich

PRAYER. *Dearest Jesus, I trust in Your words of love and comfort. There are times, however, when I am afraid. Strengthen me that I may trust You completely, on good days and bad.*

E glad in the Lord and rejoice . . . ; shout for joy, all you upright of heart.

—Ps 32:11

REFLECTION. The Lord is aware that life, with its many sorrows, is a penance. One of the greatest sorrows is not to be a joyful, holy Saint.

We pine for paradise; this yearning for God will always be with us.

PRAYER. *Lord, no matter what I do, it is only through You that I do it. Enable me to work as if all depended on me and pray as if all depended on You—and to be joyful in the process.*

OU will be hated by all because of My Name, but whoever stands firm to the end will be saved.

—Mt 10:22

REFLECTION. Vince Lombardi, the late great football coach of the Green Bay Packers, said, "A winner never quits and a quitter never wins."

Hang in there. Stand firm in the strength of the Lord, even if people speak against you because of your faith.

PRAYER. *Jesus, You have dominion over the whole earth. Enable me to see Your loving hand behind all events and to accept each as an opportunity to rely on Your strength.*

 HE Lord of hosts says, ". . . I will judge you, each according to his ways."

—Ezek 18:30

REFLECTION. Grace builds on nature, so we must all do our share to make this a better world.

Believe that you are responsible for your thoughts and actions. Accept the fact that you are what you are today largely because of your own choices. As you move into the future choose wisely.

PRAYER. *Father in heaven, help me to know myself that I may not blame others for my shortcomings. I want to walk humbly with You in the journey of life. Be my guide.*

HEN you give alms, do not let your left hand know what your right hand is doing. Your alms-giving must be done in secret. **MAY 14**
—Mt 6:3-4

REFLECTION. "One little deed, done against natural inclinations for God's sake . . . has in it power outbalancing all the dust and chaff of mere profession." —*Cardinal Newman*

Success is measured by our capacity to love, and often our capacity to love is measured by our ability to be humble.

PRAYER. *Lord, You said, "Learn from Me for I am meek and humble of heart." Teach me how to be humble without becoming a doormat.*

WOMAN in labor suffers anguish because her hour has come. But when her baby is born, she no longer recalls the suffering because of her joy that she has brought a child into the world. **MAY 15**
—Jn 16:21

REFLECTION. You cannot get rid of the worries of this world or of the questionings of the intellect, but you can laugh at them. Laugh at yourself and then think of God.

In the simple relation you have with God by prayer, it is as though you are in the center of a wheel where the noise of the revolving circumference does not matter. —*Abbot John Chapman*

PRAYER. *Holy Spirit of joy and peace, I need Your good cheer. So often I feel I am in the dark. Calm my spirit. Put a smile on my face.*

TEACH [the Faith] to your children and to their children after them.

—Deut 4:9

REFLECTION. I believe, I profoundly believe in a better world. It is for me much more real than this miserly fantasy that we devour and call life; it is always before my eyes.

I believe with all the powers of my conviction, and after so many struggles, so many studies, and so many proofs, it is the supreme consolation of my soul! —*Victor Hugo*

PRAYER. *Almighty Father, give me a passion to spread the Good News. The knowledge that You are unchanging Love fills me with consolation and joy.*

———

SAY to those with fearful hearts. "Take courage, do not be afraid. Behold, your God will . . . save you." —Isa 35:4

MAY 17

REFLECTION. Meister Eckhart used to advise his followers "to suffer God."

He meant that we should bear lovingly with God, even if we do not understand Him. We should trust Him, when He is silent, even if His silence baffles us.

PRAYER. *Grant me, O Lord, the bravery I need to be Your true follower. I am so easily discouraged. I place my trust in You for You alone are holy.*

75

FIGHT the good fight of the faith. . . . Take hold of the life eternal to which you have been called. —1 Tim 6:12

MAY 18

REFLECTION. In the mystical revelations of Bl. Henry Suso written in 1327, God said: "Do you not know that I wish only what is best for you, more earnestly than you do yourself?"

"If you were forever bathed in the heavenly dew of spiritual sweetness . . . this would not oblige Me to you nor make Me your debtor as does loving suffering or resignation in hardship."

PRAYER. *Lord, I praise You for Your wisdom. Help me to love the Cross and give me the wisdom to see suffering as a hidden blessing.*

YOU will keep them in perfect peace whose mind is fixed on You, because they trust You. —Isa 26:3

MAY 19

REFLECTION. I wrote the following when I was feeling low:

"I am not alone for God is always with me.
I am not afraid for God is protecting me.
I am forgiven everything for God is loving me.
I will bear good fruit for God is helping me.
I will persevere for God is sustaining me.
I will be saved for God is calling me."

PRAYER. *Dear Jesus, You know that I love You. I am trying day by day to rise above my petty fears, and little by little I am succeeding. Thank You for Your grace.*

REJOICE with those who rejoice. Weep with those who weep. Be of one mind toward one another.

MAY 20

—Rom 12:15-16

REFLECTION. Teilhard de Chardin spoke of suffering as the very means of return, discovery, and growth. I think he meant that death itself, and everything that leads up to it, is a doorway to a new age. Today many people cannot face suffering. They retreat from it because they do not understand it. Consequently, many become mentally sick. It is better to face the pain as Jesus did.

Christ turned His suffering into an act of love.

PRAYER. *Jesus, there are many who carry a heavier cross than I. Help me to weep with them, so that later, we may rejoice together with You in Your Kingdom.*

ABOVE all, maintain the fervor of your love for one another, because love covers a multitude of sins.

MAY 21

—1 Pet 4:8

REFLECTION. Jesus taught us to go out of ourselves and unite with others in bonds of caring. Do not let your possessions hold you back. He said, "Come and follow Me."

The Gospel injunction of renunciation is at the heart of all Christian teaching.

PRAYER. *Dear Lord, You have said that much will be forgiven for those who love much. Thank You for this teaching. I need it.*

OME, you who are blessed by My Father, inherit the Kingdom prepared for you. . . . For I was hungry and you gave Me something to eat; I was thirsty and you gave Me something to drink.

—Mt 25:35

REFLECTION. Most people cannot reach out to the poor because they are afraid—of them, their neighborhoods, even their children.

When fear begins to breed division, it becomes a spiritual problem. We are victims of our own fears when we allow them to shape our decisions and our personality.

PRAYER. *Lord, You alone can give me the grace to see beyond my present fears. Help me to be compassionate to those in need so that I do not dwell so much on my own miseries.*

 ND whenever you stand in prayer, forgive whatever grievance you have against anybody, so that your Father in heaven may forgive your wrongs too.

—Mk 11:25

REFLECTION. Forgiveness bears good fruit, and certainly banishes resentment, the enemy of joy.

When resentment and guilt are dropped, things begin to happen—both to the forgiver and to the forgiven. It is like opening a dam and letting the water flow. Power is released.

PRAYER. *Holy Spirit, soul of my soul, help me to forgive everyone who has ever hurt me. Liberate me from my resentment and from my hurt that I may have life, and life in abundance.*

ESUS replied, "Blessed . . . are those **MAY** who hear the Word of God and put it into practice." —Lk 11:28 **24**

REFLECTION. Jesus asks us to act upon His words, and we know we can because, with God's help, everything is possible.

The trick is getting yourself in a frame of mind where you can truly enter into His life, and take positive constructive action. It is not enough to believe, one must also obey. That means one must act.

PRAYER. *Jesus, Lord of my life, open my eyes and ears that I may drink in Your wisdom and grow in Your love.*

 NDEED, in our hearts we felt that we were **MAY** under a sentence of death. This was designed to show us that we must put our trust not in ourselves but in God. —2 Cor 1:9 **25**

REFLECTION. Relief comes to those who call upon the Name of the Lord at the first sign of trouble. First feel the pain and own it. Then turn it over to the Lord. You are never alone.

Sit back and be glad because of His strength. All will be well.

PRAYER. *Dear Jesus, I call on You right now. Thank You for being my Protector.*

RESENTMENT kills the fool, and indignation slays the simple.

—Job 5:2

MAY 26

REFLECTION. When a person gets angry with God, God's nature does not change. God is Unchanging Love. He always returns good for evil, and love for hatred.

We, on the other hand, establish our own criteria for God. If He does not do as we expect, we walk away from Him. Ultimately it is we who create our own hell as we withdraw from God's love. The flower needs the sun.

PRAYER. *Let Your Light shine on me, O Lord, deliver me from my resentments. There are times when I do not think I can ever get over these feelings, but I know You will heal me.*

GOD . . . takes pleasure in seeing His servants in peace.

—Ps 35:27

MAY 27

REFLECTION. Is it not true that a good father will delight in the well-being of his children?

So it is with God. He delights in your well-being, and expresses deep concern over your sadness. Lift up your heart and have a new confidence.

PRAYER. *Our Father, Who art in heaven, hallowed be Thy name. I place my trust in You. In Your Will I find my peace.*

B E all of one mind, sympathetic, filled with love for one another, and humble. MAY
—1 Pet 3:8
28

REFLECTION. Being of one mind with God is the goal. You reach it by showing love to those whom He loves.

Since that includes everyone, teach yourself to be compassionate as a permanent trait of character, or at least pray for the grace.

PRAYER. *Dear Jesus, You call us to live on earth as Your family lives in the Kingdom of Heaven. I sincerely want to do that; show me the way.*

L ORD, teach us to pray, just as John [the Baptist] taught his disciples. MAY
—Lk 11:1
29

REFLECTION. Pray in order to give yourself to God. Begin wherever you find yourself. Make any acts you want to make and feel you ought to make, but do not force yourself into feelings of any kind.

Just give yourself to God and if you cannot think of what to say, beg Him to have mercy on you and offer Him all your distractions.

—*Abbot John Chapman*

PRAYER. *Lord, I am going to give myself to You right now. I feel stupid at times when I pray because I do not exactly know what to say. So I will offer You my stupidity, and trust that You will be pleased with my humble efforts.*

HEN Jesus told them a parable about the need for them to pray always and never to lose heart.

—Lk 18:1

MAY
30

REFLECTION. Prayer is the breath of the Mystical Body. It is conversation with God. It is the expression of the soul's love and its striving toward the Father.

—Pope Paul VI

PRAYER. *O Lord Jesus, send Your Spirit into my heart so that I may join my voice to Yours as I give glory to the Father. Let me rest in Your Presence and be at peace.*

OW beautiful are the feet of those who preach the Gospel of peace, of those who bring glad tidings.

—Rom 10:15

MAY
31

REFLECTION. We all have the duty to bring glad tidings to those in need.

Let us draw nearer to Jesus so we can learn to be humble messengers of joy.

PRAYER. *Dear Lord, I do not know about the beauty of my feet, but I do know about the joy I feel when I cheer someone on who has been downcast. Help me to be a messenger of joy all the days of my life.*

82

ET us love one another, for love is from God. And everyone who loves is born of God. —1 Jn 4:7

JUNE 1

REFLECTION. Living the Gospel joyfully is really a matter of loving others. Joy follows love.

To be born of God is to be a creature of love and joy. His life flows in us and through us.

PRAYER. *Lord God, Heavenly King, fill me with Your substance and life that I may radiate Your joy wherever I go.*

———————

 F you ask anything of Me in My Name, I will do it. —Jn 14:14

JUNE 2

REFLECTION. I think this quote would be more complete if we remembered the words of Jesus in the Agony of the Garden, "Not My Will but Yours be done."

You would not expect the Lord to kill someone for you would you? Ask for what is good.

PRAYER. *Dear Jesus, I need so many things, and You know what they are before I ask. Take all my petitions and bring them to the Father. I will accept whatever He allows to happen to me.*

83

ET your main focus be on His Kingdom, **JUNE**
and these things will be given to you.
—Lk 12:31 **3**

REFLECTION. Seeking the Kingdom of God is
the essential thing. How do you do that?

You do it not by wishing, but by willing it.
Living in harmony with God and neighbor
brings a kind of peace this world cannot give.

PRAYER. *Thank You, Jesus, for teaching me
the secret of joy. Seeking Your Kingdom
above all else is the key.*

 AY the God of patience and of **JUNE**
comfort grant you to be of one
mind toward each other.—Rom 15:5 **4**

REFLECTION. To be of one mind with God may
take a little time, but it is a goal that will test
your charity and humility.

If you try to make progress, step by step,
you will please the Lord. In the meantime, do
not be too hard on yourself. God is patient.

PRAYER. *Jesus, You know my coming and my
going. Your patience with me is greatly appreciated. Now help me to be patient with
others.*

AM the Light of the world. Everyone who follows Me will not walk in darkness, but will have the light of life. —Jn 8:12

JUNE 5

REFLECTION. A true Christian life is joyful, and it is centered on Jesus. A joyful life can be pursued in many ways, but Christians have a special advantage in knowing where to look.

We look to Jesus. Our faith in Him gives us a knowledge and an understanding of ourselves and the world around us, a knowledge illuminated by His light.

PRAYER. *You, O Lord, are the Light. In You I find my way, my strength, and my joy.*

 E are regarded . . . as sorrowful, and yet we are always rejoicing; as poor, and yet we make many rich; as having nothing, and yet we possess everything.

JUNE 6

—2 Cor 6:8-10

REFLECTION. Stand fast in your faith. Speak up, write that letter, resist evil—at work, at meetings, in school, wherever the anti-God movement is promoted. Protect your children.

Strengthen the bonds of love in your home. Pray for God's help in all circumstances. Care about one another. Listen to one another.

PRAYER. *Holy Spirit, Soul of my soul, give me the spirit of courage. Help me to live in Your love that I may experience Your joy.*

B E happy. . . . Banish anxiety from your heart and cast off trouble from your presence. —Eccl 11:9-10

REFLECTION. The word "happiness" comes from the Greek and means "without pining"—that is, longing for nothing.

God is completely happy, and it is His very nature to share Himself with us. It pleases Him to help us partake of His happiness.

PRAYER. *Dear Jesus, deliver me from fear and worry. Teach me to trust You with my whole heart. In You I find the happiness I long for, and the peace I need.*

B Y this is My Father glorified, that you bear much fruit and become My disciples. —Jn 15:8

REFLECTION. When we preach the Gospel we preach it with our lives. We reveal our love of Jesus by what we do and say. Go therefore and teach all nations.

Be messengers of joy. Joy and love are the infallible signs of the presence of the Holy Spirit.

PRAYER. *Father, Son, and Holy Spirit, help me to bear good fruit by spreading Your joy and love in the world.*

HEN Jesus saw the crowds, He went up on the mountain. After He was seated, His disciples gathered around Him. Then He began to teach as follows: "Blessed. . . ."

JUNE
9

—Mt 5:1-2

REFLECTION. The eight Beatitudes are considered folly by many who follow the wisdom of this world.

In reality, however, they are the blueprint of a true Christian humanism. People learn to care for one another day by day.

PRAYER. *Heavenly Father, help me to understand these words of Jesus. Enable me to be meek and humble of heart, as Jesus was.*

AVE courage. It is I. Do not be afraid.

—Mk 6:51

JUNE
10

REFLECTION. Even trouble has its purpose. It leads to prayer.

In times of stress we are once again reunited with the Lord. There is always hope in the knowledge of His love.

PRAYER. *Dear Jesus, as the winds stirred up the lake, You came to the frightened Apostles, walking on the water. Help me to see You whenever the turbulence of my life overwhelms me. Enable me to take courage and be of good cheer.*

IVE thanks in all circumstances. For this is the Will of God for you in Christ Jesus. —1 Thes 5:18

JUNE 11

REFLECTION. Cultivate a grateful heart by continually thanking God.

You cannot keep your mind on God all day long, but you can make an intention in the morning that every breath you take will be a prayer of thanksgiving.

PRAYER. *Almighty Father, I know that a grateful heart chases away sadness and fear. Keep my heart happy and grateful.*

 OVE, therefore, is the fulfillment of the Law. —Rom 13:10

JUNE 12

REFLECTION. I learned that Christ's love in me impels me to show kindness when I want to be selfish. It is His love that induces me to sacrifice my time and comfort, when others reach out to me.

It is no big deal, just a part of life. However imperfectly I perform, I know it is the Lord working in me. I am a channel of His love.

PRAYER. *Jesus, You are my strength and my joy. Thank You for helping me live the Gospel joyfully.*

88

LOVERS of Your Law have much peace, nor is it a stumbling block for them.

JUNE 13

—Ps 119:165

REFLECTION. St. Anthony of Padua (whom we celebrate today) was a lover of God's Will and a man of peace.

He was a priest and a Doctor of the Church, as well as a miracle worker. He was also a man of deep prayer.

PRAYER. *Dear Jesus, teach me to be still in Your loving presence. Help me to love Your Holy Will, even if at times it is difficult. In Your Will is my peace.*

 DURING this period of time, He went onto the mountain to pray, and He spent the entire night in prayer to God.

JUNE 14

—Lk 6:12

REFLECTION. The soul needs silence and solitude to draw from God's immense power. Like a battery in need of a charge, we need to plug into God's power.

Without prayer there will be no spiritual perception, no spiritual energy.

PRAYER. *Help me, Father, to be sincere in my effort to give myself to You alone. Bless me with Your love.*

CHEERFUL heart enjoys a continual feast. —Prov 15:15

REFLECTION. Some people are put off by the emphasis on good cheer, and I understand that.

They know that the real life of the Spirit has little to do with emotional enjoyment sought for its own sake, even if it is enjoyment of the loftiest kind. But that does not mean our religion should make us stodgy.

PRAYER. *O Lord, help me to understand that You love a cheerful giver. Grant me the grace of a cheerful heart.*

ET each one give . . . not grudgingly. . . for God loves a cheerful giver. —2 Cor 9:7

REFLECTION. We are a privileged people. Our goal is heaven, and with Divine help we can make it; in fact we believe eternal life has already begun here on earth. Be grateful for this gift.

Rejoice in the Risen Lord and be glad.

PRAYER. *Dear Jesus, You alone have the power to quell my fears. Help me to stay focused on heaven and rejoice always in the knowledge of Your love.*

PRAY for those who mistreat you. If anyone strikes you on one cheek, offer him the other cheek as well. —Lk 6:28-29

JUNE 17

REFLECTION. Charity is at the heart of Christian perfection; charity is human love touched by grace.

Love flows from person to person or it does not flow at all. It is not communicated by institutions or organizations but by people.

PRAYER. *Lord, Your wisdom is beyond me. To return good for evil is not my way of doing things, but I bow to Your Will. All I need is a ton of grace precisely at those moments when I want to strike out in anger.*

GO forth, therefore, and make disciples. . . . —Mt 28:19

JUNE 18

REFLECTION. When we speak of going forth we focus on Jesus. The Church is Christ living in His Mystical Body on earth today.

Just as Jesus had a mission, so too does the Church. We are commissioned to be other Christs, and do what He did.

PRAYER. *Lord, teach me to be patient and kind. I hope for the best when I trust in Your power. Give me the heart to go forward with courage.*

FORGETTING what is behind me and straining forward to what lies ahead, I press on toward the finishing line to win the heavenly prize to which God has called me in Christ Jesus. —Phil 3:13-14

JUNE 19

REFLECTION.

Whether by a healthy child, a garden patch,
  or a redeemed social condition;
To know even one life has
breathed easier because you lived.
This is to have succeeded.

—*Ralph Waldo Emerson*

PRAYER. *Lord, I do not ask for success. I ask only to be faithful to You. Help me to do my share to make this a better world.*

I WAS ill and you took care of Me. —Mt 25:36

JUNE 20

REFLECTION. Thomas Carlyle, the historian, was right when he said:

"Empires fall or civilizations decline, not necessarily through some colossal criminality, but from multitudinous cases of petty betrayal or individual neglect."

PRAYER. *Dear Jesus, help me to minister to those in need. Enlighten my mind that I may see You living in my neighbor.*

ARTHA, Martha, you are anxious about many things, yet only one thing is necessary. —Lk 10:41-42

JUNE 21

REFLECTION. To love and listen, these are the marks of a true disciple.

Love is the necessary thing, but listening to wisdom helps one to distinguish between love in dreams and love in action.

PRAYER. *Dearest Lord, I want to give generously of myself without counting the cost, but I am so often a coward. Teach me to be at peace within myself and free me from needless worry.*

 OU must regard yourselves as being dead to sin and alive for God in Christ Jesus. —Rom 6:11

JUNE 22

REFLECTION. Paul's greatest intuition was his identification with the Christ-life within his soul. He is led, strengthened, and inspired to want what Jesus wants. Remember his words: "It is no longer I who live, but it is Christ Who lives in me" (Gal 2:20).

This act of surrender gave him a far different personality from the one he had before he was knocked off his horse in Damascus.

PRAYER. *Jesus, meek and humble of heart, make my heart like unto Yours.*

93

THE word of the Lord is true; all His works are trustworthy.

—Ps 33:4

REFLECTION.

Thank the Lord for His truth.

Thank Him for your wonderful body,
   mind, heart, and soul.

Thank Him for our beautiful planet,
   for the stars and the sky,
   our human brethren and sisters,
   our friends and the animals,
   our sisters the plants and flowers.

—*Robert Mueller*

PRAYER. *Father, I see the splendor of Your creation. I thank You for everything that lives and has being.*

SOUGHT the Lord, and He answered me; He set me free from all my fears.

—Ps 34:5

REFLECTION. Joy destroys fear. Fear is the enemy of joy. If you cling to fear and self-pity you will lose your joy.

Therefore, ask the Lord to banish fear from your heart.

PRAYER. *Deliver me, O Lord, from all needless worry and fear. Flood my soul with joy. Teach me to smile in Your presence.*

ING to the Lord a new song of praise in the assembly of His faithful ones.

—Ps 149:1

JUNE 25

REFLECTION. Lift up your heart, have a new confidence. Say yes to life and live cheerfully, enthusiastically.

The Lord deserves our cheers and our songs of praise.

PRAYER. *O Lord, help me to realize that the Liturgy is a precious gift You have entrusted to Your Church. May I always participate in the Liturgy in a joyful manner.*

HE meek shall increase their joy in the Lord.

—Isa 29:19

JUNE 26

REFLECTION. I call. I call you. I know that this is bold of me, maybe even vain, possibly a bit inconvenient. But I must call out as Jesus did: come with me.

The Lord asks for a precious gift, the gift of yourself, a sacrifice without limitations. Be humble and enjoy the Lord.

PRAYER. *Dear Jesus, I know that if I truly submit to You in meekness, You will shower me with blessings. Give me courage, Lord, and I will be Your obedient servant.*

YE has not seen, ear has not heard, nor has the human heart imagined what God has prepared for those who love Him.

—1 Cor 2:9

JUNE
27

REFLECTION. A life rooted in God is one filled with His reality. It is a life where God's Spirit does the leading.

In such a state of surrender we might find ourselves drawn to a place we never fancied for ourselves.

PRAYER. *Lord, take me where You will. My heart is restless until it rests in You. Be my guide and my salvation.*

N everything, deal with others as you would like them to deal with you.

—Mt 7:12

JUNE
28

REFLECTION. The slothful person does not want to give up his comfort. The fear of being disturbed makes the slothful person extremely secretive and lonely.

Sloth leads to selfishness. Love withers in a slothful person.

PRAYER. *Jesus, help me to overcome my laziness. With a little effort I can extend myself to make my neighbor's life a little more cheerful.*

E pray always for you, that our God . . . may by His power fulfill every good purpose of yours and every act prompted by your faith.

JUNE 29

—2 Thes 1:11

REFLECTION. The feast of the Apostles Peter and Paul reminds us of the prayers and sacrifices of those who have gone before us.

The Apostles were outstanding witnesses of Jesus Christ. You are a witness too.

PRAYER. *Lord, let me witness to the reality of Your love, by being a kind and gentle person, so that my joy will be full in serving others.*

VERYONE in the crowd was trying to touch Him, because power came forth from Him and healed them all.

JUNE 30

—Lk 6:19

REFLECTION. To this very day power goes out from Jesus and people are cured. There are many kinds of cures, however. Some take a long time to understand. Sometimes the pain of life makes a person more humble and pliable.

Since we will all need a childlike spirit to enter the Kingdom, maybe God is doing us a favor by not giving us exactly what we want when we want it. Maybe He is preparing us for a greater gift.

PRAYER. *Dear Jesus, I certainly need You and I want to please You. Please cure me of my bodily ills as well as my spiritual sickness. I trust You to heal me in Your own way.*

THE blind receive their sight, the lame walk, those who have leprosy are cured, the deaf hear, the dead are raised to life, and the poor have the Good News proclaimed to them.

JULY 1

—Mt 11:5

REFLECTION. People of old believed that blindness or leprosy was a sign of God's punishment for sin. Jesus overturned that belief and paid a great price for it.

They thought He was changing the tradition, when in fact He was challenging them to believe in God's love.

PRAYER. *Lord Jesus, I put my trust in You not in old wives' tales. I believe in God's unchanging love, and nothing can undermine my confidence in this truth.*

ET your light shine before others so that they may see your good works and glorify your Father in heaven.

JULY 2

—Mt 5:16

REFLECTION. Jesus empowers you to bring a life-giving light to this world, a light that will help dispel the darkness around you.

You may not see your spiritual aura, but it is there. You may not be able to judge your own light, but others can.

PRAYER. *Jesus, I know Your light shines in me and through me. I offer Your light to everyone I meet when I smile at them.*

E loved the Lord with his whole heart and daily sang His praises.

JULY 3

—Sir 47:8

REFLECTION. St. Augustine suggests that people pray twice when they sing.

Even this suggestion fails to move many in the church congregation. But we do hum and whistle and sing when we are happy. Offer your happiness to God.

PRAYER. *You, Lord, are the Bread of Life, I praise You and sing hymns to Your glory.*

 CHEERFUL heart is excellent medicine, whereas a downcast spirit leaves one debilitated.

JULY 4

—Prov 17:22

REFLECTION. On Independence Day we celebrate the birth of our nation. Lift up your heart and join the celebration.

Rosalind Russell, the late actress, once said, "Laughter is like air and water to me." During the last 16 years of her life she suffered the ravages of rheumatoid arthritis, but "Roz" kept that cheerful spirit alive. "Whatever comes to me," she said, "I will accept. Faith in God and ourselves gives us peace and the assurance we will overcome."

PRAYER. *Dear Lord, I pray for the grace to accept the things I cannot change. Give me a cheerful heart that I may smile all the way home.*

Y heart says, "Seek HIs face." Your face, Lord, do I seek.

JULY 5

—Ps 27:8

REFLECTION. St. Augustine wrote:

"The entire life of a good Christian is in fact an exercise of holy desire. You do not yet see what you long for, but the very act of desiring prepares you so that when He comes, you may see and be utterly satisfied."

PRAYER. *Lord Jesus, come into my heart. I am an unworthy vessel, but I long to be Your resting place. I know that even now You are with me. I have knocked and You have answered me.*

 E may say with confidence: "The Lord is my helper. I will not be afraid."

JULY 6

—Heb 13:6

REFLECTION. Jesus was sent by the Father to tell us that God loves us and wants to save us.

If you develop a taste for God now, and allow it to grow into a flaming desire, your soul will expand and magnify your love. God is aware of every movement in your heart. In fact, He leads you to new heights precisely through your own desires.

PRAYER. *Dear Lord, as I contemplate Your love for me, my heart begins to leap for joy. This joy is rooted in my love for You.*

ET us therefore love, because God first loved us.

—1 Jn 4:19

JULY 7

REFLECTION. If all the people of the world were symbolized by 100 people in one room, two-thirds would be poor. Of the 66 poor people, about 35 would suffer from hunger and malnutrition, living in substandard housing or actually be homeless. Only 50 out of 100 would be able to read and write, and only one out of 100 would have a college education.

If you really want to love God with all your heart, think of others.

PRAYER. *Teach me to be sensitive to the needs of others, Lord, that I may experience the joy of loving You in each of them.*

"T is finished."

—Jn 19:30

JULY 8

REFLECTION. On the Cross, Jesus does not merely offer His pain and His life. He offers all human pain, the entire process of evolution, plus "all the harnessed power" of our lives.

Nothing is wasted, nothing is fruitless.

PRAYER. *Jesus, I unite my suffering with Yours. Use me as You see fit. It gives me joy to know that nothing is wasted.*

101

REJOICING in the Lord is your strength.
—Neh 8:10

**JULY
9**

REFLECTION. If that Scripture quote simply said, "The Lord is your strength," it would not be difficult to understand, would it? But God is like a three faceted diamond: Love, Joy, and Peace.

God is not only love, God is joy. Therefore, the Joy of the Lord is God Himself. Let the Lord fill you with love, joy, and peace.

PRAYER. *Thank You, Lord, for Your gift. Help me to return the gift by giving myself right back to You.*

LET the mountains shout for joy before the Lord. He comes to govern the earth with justice.

**JULY
10**

—Ps 98:8-9

REFLECTION. Joy is not attained through self-indulgence, or a life of religious posturing. It is certainly not found in anxious activity. Joy flows from our relationship with God.

Joy comes from the Lord. He communicates it to us. We merely respond to the promptings of His Spirit.

PRAYER. *Fill me, Jesus, with Your joyful Spirit that I may truly know Your strength. Lift up my heart with gladness.*

FOR the Lord hears the needy and does not turn His back on captives.

—Ps 69:34

JULY 11

REFLECTION. Jean Vanier said:

"I have learned more about the Gospels from handicapped people, those on the margins of our society, those who have been crushed and hurt, than I have from the wise and prudent."

PRAYER. *Dear Lord, I want to see Your face in the least of my brothers and sisters. Teach me the secret of caring about the plight of the poorest of the poor.*

LEARN from Me, for I am meek and humble of heart.

—Mt 11:29

JULY 12

REFLECTION. Jean Vanier reminds us all how much we need to learn from the meek and the humble of this world.

It is only when we accept our own littleness that we can learn to open ourselves to the Spirit of Love that Jesus promised.

PRAYER. *Holy Spirit of Love, give me the childlike spirit that Jesus had. Help me to see You in the little ones of this world.*

H E must keep this book with him and read it all the days of his life that he may learn to revere the Lord.

JULY
13

—Deut 17:19

REFLECTION. Read widely, expand your horizons in literature. The Latin orator Cicero said:

"Books add to our joy in prosperity and provide refuge and comfort in adversity; they give pleasure at home and advancement abroad; they pass the night hours with us, and accompany us on the road."

PRAYER. *Dear Jesus, I do not need a Latin scholar to learn wisdom. Thank You for my intelligence, and Your grace.*

E doers of the word and not just hearers who only deceive themselves.

JULY
14

—Jas 1:22

REFLECTION. The desire to be coddled, to live without effort, goes back to infancy. It is a natural tendency in all of us. Those who habitually fall prey to escapism develop what psychiatrists call a passive-dependent personality.

It is probably the most common of all psychiatric disorders. People with this disorder are so busy looking for love in all the wrong places that they have no energy left to love."

PRAYER. *Help me to know myself, O Lord. Give me the courage to think of others and then to act on my good intentions.*

TRUE friend is one who loves you at all times, and a brother is born to help you endure adversity.

JULY 15

—Prov 17:17

REFLECTION. By the wonderful gift of faith we know that God cares about each one of us personally.

To lose sight of this truth is to narrow our chances for happiness. Who wants to live like a poor helpless creature?

PRAYER. *O God, I know You are my Friend. Let me replace all negative thoughts and feelings with happy, positive ones. May I radiate confidence in Your love.*

ET us not love in word or speech but in deed and action.

JULY 16

—1 Jn 3:18

REFLECTION. Love is the real measuring rod for success. Nobel Peace Prize winner, Mother Teresa of Calcutta, once said:

"When we come face to face with God, we are going to be judged on love, not on how much we have done but how much love we have put into our actions."

PRAYER. *Dear Lord, I need Your strength to keep on keeping on. Thank You for Your unfailing support.*

OU are the light of the world. A city built upon a mountain cannot be hidden from view. —Mt 5:14

REFLECTION. What an astonishing statement! And yet Jesus proclaimed it. You and I are like beacons of light in a world of darkness.

We live in what Pope John Paul II called the culture of death. Let us all combine our efforts to be a force for life. It is better to light one candle than to curse the darkness.

PRAYER. *Lord, I am ablaze with Your Light. Let my light shine for all to see, so that I may bear good fruit for all eternity.*

HAVE learned to be content with whatever I have. . . . I can do all things in Him Who strengthens me. —Phil 4:11-13

REFLECTION. You may not feel like a blaze of glory or a great Saint, but you have an inner light that no one can take from you. "Let your light shine for all to see."

In Christ all things are possible.

PRAYER. *Holy Lord, You are the Sun, I am the moon reflecting You. I believe that I am radiant in Your Light. Give me confidence to let my light shine.*

BIDE in Me, and I will abide in you. **JULY**
—Jn 15:4
19

REFLECTION. To abide in the Lord is to provide
a resting place in your heart for the indwelling
Spirit. In that way you become a temple of the
Holy Spirit.

His love informs all you do.

PRAYER. *Lord Jesus, let me begin to be a light
for others by acknowledging that Your light
shines in me. Help me to believe in You and so
become a spiritual power for good.*

ONSIDER yourself blessed, for upon **JULY**
you rests the Spirit of glory and of
God. —1 Pet 4:15 **20**

REFLECTION. Try to see your mission as a
Christian duty, a duty that does not depend on
you or your personality. It depends on your
faith in God's presence.

God is expressing His love through you. He
asks for your hands and your heart.

PRAYER. *Lord, make me an instrument of
Your peace. Where there is hatred let me
bring love, and where there is sadness, let me
bring joy.*

CHRIST did not send me to baptize but to preach the Gospel—and to do so without words of human wisdom lest the Cross of Christ be devoid of its meaning.

—1 Cor 1:17

REFLECTION. Teilhard de Chardin viewed the Cross differently from the way it is usually seen.

He saw it as a sign of human evolution, that is, a symbol of the whole process of our growth toward heaven. All the suffering and hard work of the human race over the centuries is recapitulated in Christ's Passion and Death.

PRAYER. *Grant that I may give You, Lord Jesus, my whole being, tree and fruit alike, the finished work as well as the harnessed power.* —*Teilhard de Chardin*

THE word of the Lord is true; all His works are trustworthy.

—Ps 33:4

REFLECTION. In *The Brothers Karamazov*, Dostoyevsky wrote:

"Never be frightened at your own faintheartedness in attaining love. For love in action is a harsh and dreadful thing compared with love in dreams. Love in dreams is greedy for immediate action, rapidly performed; hoping that all will be looking on applauding, as though on a stage. But active love is labor and fortitude."

PRAYER. *Dear Lord, help me not to be afraid of my weaknesses or discouraged by my revulsion at the first sign of the cross.*

IT is not the healthy who need a physician, but rather those who are sick. I have come to call not the righteous but sinners. —Mk 2:17

JULY 23

REFLECTION. Do not worry if you are not particularly joyful on any given day. Perhaps you think you are not worthy. Nonsense!

When you think about the bad things you have done in the past, it has a purifying effect. You become purer and humbler by a spirit of penance. However, you must also learn to let go of it. Turn the past over to God's mercy.

PRAYER. *Lord, You help me to see myself as I am. I know You want me to be a joyful person. Refresh my drooping spirit.*

 HERE is a time for everything. . . . A time to keep silence, and a time to speak. —Eccl 3:1, 7

JULY 24

REFLECTION. We should strive to have the spirit of true wisdom.

True wisdom enables us to know not only when and how to speak but also when and where to remain silent. Sometimes it is better to say nothing.

PRAYER. *Dear Jesus, You bore so many humiliations in silence. Help me to keep my mouth shut when I want to scream out my indignation.*

HOEVER has seen Me has seen the Father. How can you say, "Show us the Father"? Do you not believe that I am in the Father and the Father is in Me?

—Jn 14:9-10

REFLECTION. Faith is knowledge. One either knows or does not know that the supreme revelation of God is Jesus Christ. To know Jesus is to begin to understand God.

Whether or not you get daily briefings from on high is not the issue. To know Jesus is to know where to look to find the meaning of human happiness.

PRAYER. *Open my eyes, O Lord, that I may see Your glory.*

HEREFORE, if the Son sets you free, you then will be truly free.

—Jn 8:36

REFLECTION. If you want a deeper awareness of God the Father look to Jesus, look at His words and deeds. In His lifetime He reached out to the lepers, the prostitutes, the handicapped, the outcast.

He spoke of Himself as the Good Shepherd Who leaves the 99 to search for the lost one. He lays down His life for His sheep.

PRAYER. *Father, You watch over me even when I step off base. I want my own way so often. Thank You for following me when I wander off.*

I AM the Bread of Life.

—Jn 6:35

REFLECTION. Jesus called Himself the Bread of Life, and He comes to feed our hunger.

He called Himself the Resurrection and He lifts us from our fear of death by promising eternal happiness.

PRAYER. *Dear Jesus, You have shown us the Father, and in the words of St. Philip, "That is enough for us." You feed us and lift us out of our misery. Thank You for the Eucharist.*

A MEN, amen, I say to you, if you ask the Father for anything in My Name, He will give it to you. . . . Ask and you will receive, so that your joy may be complete. —Jn 16:23-24

REFLECTION. The life of Jesus teaches us that God is like a loving human father. God understood our limitations so "He gave His only begotten Son" to light our path.

We recognize Jesus as a loving person, Who cares about us.

PRAYER. *Dear Father in heaven, Jesus has given us the words of life. Help me to take hold of them and make them my own. I ask for the gift of joy. Thank You for keeping me ever by Your side.*

IVE in a manner worthy of the Lord and become fully pleasing to Him bearing fruit in every good work.

JULY 29

—Col 1:10

REFLECTION. Jesus never forced anyone to comply with His teachings. He simply asks for our obedience that our joy may be full.

All He asks is that we make a reasonable effort to be good.

PRAYER. *Lord Jesus, help me never to measure my morality by the standards of an unbelieving world. Let the Gospel be the source of my beliefs.*

 HOEVER drinks of the water that I will give them will never thirst. The water . . . will become in them a fountain of water, springing up to eternal life.

JULY 30

—Jn 4:13-14

REFLECTION. The Holy Spirit is called the Fountain of Living Waters. That means your soul has a constant supply of fresh, satisfying grace and love.

Receive this gift with a grateful heart.

PRAYER. *Lord Jesus, let me drink deeply at the fountain of Your love. Let me sate my thirst with Your life. You are the fountain of eternal life.*

LESSED are you when people reproach you, and persecute you, and speaking falsely, say all manner of evil against you for My sake. —Mt 5:11

REFLECTION. The martyrs in the days of the Roman persecutions were said to have sung to the glory of God with jubilation.

They were full of the Lord in a way that none of us could possibly imagine. They were joyful in the face of a cruel death. "Death, where is your sting?" (1 Cor 15:55).

PRAYER. *Lord Jesus, You proclaimed blessed those who suffer for the sake of justice. Let me be among those great souls. Help me to be fearless when the going gets rough.*

 MYSELF will tend My sheep. . . . I will search for the lost and bring back the strays. —Ezek 34:15-16

REFLECTION. The spirituality of St. Therese of Lisieux, can be summarized in these words: "God is nothing but love and mercy."

Therefore, instead of being offended by sinners, God seeks them out, and is willing to die for them. This is precisely what is meant by the Good News of the Gospel.

PRAYER. *Father, how wonderful it is to realize that You not only forgive but also pursue the lost sheep to rescue them. How wonderful it is to know that You are there, loving me, forgiving me, and helping me to forgive myself.*

T is not the will of your Father in heaven that a single one of these [lost sheep] should be lost.

AUG. 2

—Mt 18:12-14

REFLECTION. One day we will all stand before the Lord to be judged. What a comfort it is to know that He wants to save us more than we want to be saved.

He died that we might live in His love and His joy.

PRAYER. *Dearest Jesus, I owe You my life, I owe You everything I have. Thank You for this knowledge of Your love. It brings me such comfort and joy.*

 Y yoke is easy and My burden is light.

AUG. 3

—Mt 11:30

REFLECTION. Every burden is light when we are united to Christ. It is He Who gives us the strength to go on walking.

On the other hand, the burden of life is heavy when it is carried without Christ!

PRAYER. *Dear Lord, sharpen my mind that I may have insight. I want to focus on the positive aspects of my faith—mainly I want to focus on You. Remind me to call upon You the instant I begin feeling sorry for myself.*

TEMPTATION occurs when someone is attracted and seduced by his own desire. Then the desire conceives and gives birth to sin, and that sin, when it reaches full growth, gives birth to death.

AUG.
4

—Jas 1:14-15

REFLECTION. Desires of the heart are like seeds that grow into full-blown trees. In the beginning they do not have great power, but they grow and if not stopped their progression is inevitable.

This is true both for holy desires and unholy desires to which we give our consent.

PRAYER. *Our Father, Who art in heaven, deliver me from evil now and at the hour of my death.*

I DO not understand my own actions. For I do not do the good things that I want to do; rather, I do the bad things that I do not want to do.

AUG.
5

—Rom 7:15

REFLECTION. St. Paul admitted he was weak. His own behavior often baffled him.

Isn't this true for all of us? What a joy it is to know that even the great Saints of the Church were human.

PRAYER. *Dear Lord, help me to see the whole picture. Do not let me be too hard on myself. I trust in Your mercy and love. Whether I understand myself or not, You are there, preparing me for the banquet.*

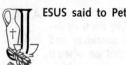

ESUS said to Peter: "Feed My sheep."
—Jn 21:17

AUG.
6

REFLECTION. Jesus asked St. Peter to make a threefold profession of his love. Three times He asked, "Do you love Me?" And three times Peter replied, "Yes, Lord, You know that I love You."

After Peter's first profession of love Jesus said, "Feed My lambs." After Peter's second and third profession, the Lord said, "Feed My sheep."

PRAYER. *Jesus, help me to be faithful to Your request. Help me to build up the faith of others by my words, my good example, and my joyful appreciation of all Your wonderful gifts.*

T is the spirit that gives life; the flesh can achieve nothing. The words that I have spoken to you are spirit and life.

AUG.
7

—Jn 6:63

REFLECTION. Some people rely too much on their own instincts and their own will.

When they get themselves into trouble, they forget to pray for God's help to change the things they can change and accept the things they cannot.

PRAYER. *Amen, Lord, I build my life on Your words. I rejoice in the knowledge of Your mercy and love.*

116

JESUS asked: . . . "Do you love Me?"
—Jn 21:15

AUG.
8

REFLECTION. Jesus asks this basic question: Do you love Me? If in your heart you can answer yes, He has promised that you will not slip from His grasp.

You may not feel very loving at any given moment, but feelings are not facts. He offers you His love, His forgiveness, and His comfort, and He never withdraws these gifts.

PRAYER. *Jesus, You are the wonder of my life. Yes, I can say it honestly. I do love You. Help me to love You more and more.*

DO not let your hearts be troubled. Place your trust in God.
—Jn 14:1

AUG.
9

REFLECTION. Worry is a normal part of life. We will never be free of the little worries that help us to keep everything in order.

But Jesus tells us to avoid the deeper worries that lead to an immobilizing fear. He assures us that we can put them aside by entrusting these problems to Him.

PRAYER. *Jesus, my Lord and my God, I abandon all my doubts and fears to You. You are the Holy One. You alone are Lord. In You I find my being and life.*

117

S we share in God's work, we urge you not to receive the grace of God in vain. —2 Cor 6:1

REFLECTION. Concentrating on God's love and protection can help prevent undue psychological anxiety.

Rejoicing because of the knowledge of God's love is in itself a kind of exorcism. St. Paul knew that anxiety does not flourish in the atmosphere of joy. He prescribes joy as a means of banishing anxiety. Our faith in the reality of God's love is of great benefit in healing and liberating the fearful spirit.

PRAYER. *Holy Spirit, You dwell within me. You are truly my partner in the journey of life. Let me feel the joy of You living deep within me.*

EAL with others as you would like them to deal with you. —Lk 6:31

AUG. 11

REFLECTION. In the area of sexuality, as in everything else, it is important to keep in mind the Golden Rule. Lust is a violation of this rule.

Lust is an inordinate desire for the gratification of one's sexual appetite. It is self-absorbed. Eventually, others are treated like objects or, worse, like slaves.

PRAYER. *Jesus, You have the wisdom that gives my life balance and holiness. Help me always to control my desires.*

118

O not be afraid. Just have faith.
—Lk 8:50

AUG.
12

REFLECTION. Fear ruins your perspective. There is a terrible fear of whites for the blacks and blacks for the whites, and there should not be.

People everywhere are really only asking to be treated like human beings. Be not afraid of your neighbor.

PRAYER. *Lord, with the help of Your grace I will put my faith in You, I will trust you. I need and I want the humility necessary to entrust all my cares to Your safekeeping.*

HE publican . . . kept striking his breast, saying, "O God, be merciful to me, a sinner."
—Lk 18:13

AUG.
13

REFLECTION. Jesus favored the publican even though others saw him as a traitor, a tax collector for the Romans.

Jesus saw that his heart was pure, and He showed him mercy.

PRAYER. *Lord, make my mind and heart like Your own. Let me see beyond first appearances. Make me an instrument of Your love.*

119

ETTER off poor, healthy, and fit than wealthy and afflicted in body. More precious than gold is health and well-being. —Sir 30:14-15

AUG. 14

REFLECTION. They say that if you have your health you have everything. That may be true in a sense, but there are a lot of healthy people who feel lonely, lost, and abandoned.

Maybe it is better to be wise, and spiritually fulfilled.

PRAYER. *Dear Jesus, I will care for my body, and I will stay as healthy as I can, but more than good health, I want Your love and Your presence in my life. With You I have all that I need.*

 GREAT sign appeared in the heavens: a woman clothed with the sun, and the moon was under her feet, and upon her head a crown of twelve stars. —Rev 12:1

AUG. 15

REFLECTION. The Assumption of Mary is a wonderful feast day for the Church. We celebrate her glory in heaven.

Jesus brought Mary home to honor her for her role in the Redemption of the human family.

PRAYER. *Dear Mary, teach me to say yes to my calling as you did to yours. Pray for me now and at the hour of my death.*

120

JESUS went about . . . curing every kind of disease and infirmity. And seeing the crowds, He had compassion on them.
—Mt 9:35-36

AUG.
16

REFLECTION. The Lord was not only sympathetic to the needs of others but also empathetic.

When He saw people in pain, He felt compassion. Compassion is taken from the Latin meaning, "to suffer with."

PRAYER. *Lord, transform me into a healing force in this world. Let me understand the pain of others better so that I may have true compassion for them as You do.*

STORE up treasure for yourselves in heaven, where neither moth nor rust destroys and where thieves cannot break in and steal. —Mt 6:20

AUG.
17

REFLECTION. Jesus taught us to find joy, not by looking for it, but by listening to His words in a spirit of humble surrender.

Enjoyment sought for its own sake is a self-centered pursuit. The Spirit does not teach us to seek joy as an end in itself. Joy is more a by-product of our intimacy with God.

PRAYER. *Dear Jesus, purify my mind that I may seek first Your Kingdom. I am not sure what that actually means, but I will put my trust in Your intimate presence; and You will guide me.*

121

HOEVER sees Me sees the One who sent Me. I have come into the world as light, so that no one who believes in Me will remain in darkness. —Jn 12:45-46

AUG. 18

REFLECTION. Jesus said, "to see Me is to see the Father." To anchor one's life in God, therefore, is to turn to Jesus.

He will unlock the mystery of joy for all of us. Knowing your purpose in life is the key.

PRAYER. *I have my mission. . . . / I am a link in a chain, a bond of connection between persons. / He has not created me for naught, / I shall do good, I shall do His work.*

—*Cardinal Newman*

VERYTHING that you do should be done in love.

—1 Cor 16:14

AUG. 19

REFLECTION. There are many battles to be fought. Governments are not too powerful to be reformed. Institutions are not too big to be changed. Positive, constructive action can overcome evil.

We firmly believe that, with the help of God, all things are possible. But always remember action without charity is not Christianity.

PRAYER. *Thank You, Jesus, for giving me the courage to remain charitable, pursing good works. May You always be my strength and my joy.*

HAT does that matter to you? You are to follow Me.

AUG. 20

—Jn 21:22

REFLECTION. Christianity is essentially an invitation. It is an invitation to a special kind of happiness and goodness, one that is rooted in the person of Jesus Christ. He invites us to follow Him. We either say yes or no.

PRAYER. *Dear Lord, I hear Your call, and I will follow You. Your words are a source of wisdom and light. Give me the courage I need to follow You all the days of my life.*

 HE entire Law can be summed up in a single commandment: "You shall love your neighbor as yourself."

AUG. 21

—Gal 5:14

REFLECTION. Teaching the Christian view of reality is best done by living it. We instruct others best by our loving actions, and then our words have the ring of truth.

Teaching is not so much communicating a list of definitions. Teaching has the more pragmatic goal of helping others to live life as God created us to live it, joyfully.

PRAYER. *Maker of heaven and earth, I am Your humble child. I want to obey Your supreme commandment—to love and be loved. Help me to overcome my selfishness.*

LESSED are those who are persecuted in the cause of justice, for theirs is the Kingdom of Heaven. —Mt 5:10

AUG. 22

REFLECTION. Believing in the Beatitudes is not fashionable, because it leads to trouble. Ridicule can be stinging; being called a bleeding heart, a do-gooder, is not enjoyable.

Everyone working for human rights has been maligned at one time or another. They are called fools. But is imitating the Lord foolishness? Was Jesus a fool for obeying the Father?

PRAYER. *Jesus, Son of the Father, You suffered humiliation and death in following Your Father's Will. Help me to be fearless in the cause of justice.*

UST as a branch cannot bear fruit by itself unless it remains attached to the vine, so you cannot bear fruit unless you abide in Me. I am the vine, you are the branches. —Jn 15:4-5

AUG. 23

REFLECTION. These words of Jesus contain the essence of His message and the secret of our joy. His life is joy itself.

Jesus teaches us that God loved us first, and He created us for a particular purpose in life. Each one of us has a job to do that nobody else in the world can do.

PRAYER. *Dear Lord, teach me how to use my life, humble as it is, for Your glory. Help me to become a conduit of Your love.*

TAKE heart . . . your sins are forgiven. **AUG.**
—Mt 9:2 **24**

REFLECTION. Before Jesus said to the paralytic,
"Take up your bed and walk," He said, "Take
heart, son, your sins are forgiven." Healing and
forgiveness are continually combined in the
Gospels.

We are paralyzed until we accept— really
accept—the fact that God forgives us. Once
we do, we are freed to love, forgive, and accept ourselves. Then the joy of healing begins.

PRAYER. *Thank You, Lord, for Your healing in
my life. I am like the paralytic, and You have
made me whole.*

LESSED are you who are poor, for the **AUG.**
Kingdom of God is yours.
—Lk 6:20 **25**

REFLECTION. How to live the Christian life?
That is the question.

How to live and receive love in communion
with others? How to forgive those who offend
us? How to pray to the Father with Jesus in
the Holy Spirit? How to go out to those in
need, without looking for praise or thanks?
All this takes meekness and humility.

PRAYER. *Father, I want to be poor in spirit so
that I may live the Christian life fully. This is
the only true happiness worth pursuing.*

EVILDOERS simply cannot understand justice, but those who seek the Lord understand it completely. **AUG. 26**

—Prov 28:5

REFLECTION. Excesses often mar high-sounding goals. In his encyclical *Rich in Mercy*, Pope John Paul II alluded to this problem:

"It is obvious in fact that in the name of an alleged justice (for example, historical or class justice) the neighbor is sometimes destroyed, killed, deprived of liberty, or stripped of fundamental human rights." The history of atheistic Marxism is filled with such abuses.

PRAYER. *Dear God, make me wise so that I may see what is right and just, and make me childlike that I may put others before myself.*

WHAT I say to you in the dark, proclaim in the daylight, and what you hear whispered, shout from the housetops. **AUG. 27** —Mt 10:27

REFLECTION. Jesus committed to His followers the main task of preaching the Gospel. How? In three ways—by our prayers, our words, and our actions.

In prayer we receive power; in our words and actions, we give it away. It is like breathing in and breathing out.

PRAYER. *Lord, fill my mind with knowledge and my heart with love, and then help me to give it all away.*

126

HOEVER does not love Me does not keep My words.

—Jn 14:24

AUG. 28

REFLECTION. Jesus came to bring joy, but this joy is the consequence of obedience to His advice and His commands.

He asks us most emphatically to love one another because when we do, life will flow beautifully. When we do not, the suffering begins.

PRAYER. *Give me the grace, O Lord, to follow You with a childlike spirit. I want to do Your Will. Give me the courage to carry out my good intentions.*

 F you are reviled for the Name of Christ, consider yourself blessed, for upon you rests the Spirit of glory and of God.

—1 Pet 4:14

AUG. 29

REFLECTION. To have the Spirit of God resting on you is the greatest compliment you can receive.

If it comes from someone who intends to punish you in some way for your beliefs, so be it. It is still a compliment.

PRAYER. *Father, help me to understand this mystery. Teach me how to accept my pain with courage, even as I seek healing and relief. I offer all my sufferings and humiliations in a spirit of reparation, and with the help of Your grace. I promise obedience and love.*

UR citizenship is in heaven, and from there we await our Savior, the Lord Jesus Christ. He will transform our lowly bodies so that they will be conformed to His glorified body by the power that also enables Him to make all things subject to Himself.

AUG. 30

—Phil 3:20-21

REFLECTION. St. Paul pleads with us to remain courageous.

We are not yet Saints, but we are Saints in training. Why not be brave? Goodness is its own reward.

PRAYER. *Lord Jesus, with You at my side, I can do all things. You are my strength and my joy.*

OPE does not disappoint, because the charity of God is poured forth in our hearts by the Holy Spirit Who has been given to us.

AUG. 31

—Rom 5:5

REFLECTION. The charity or love of God flows like a fountain. It pours out living waters to you all day long.

Mentally, keep a small pitcher close by and draw from it throughout the day. It will refresh you, and all you meet.

PRAYER. *Come, Holy Spirit, fill the heart of this faithful one, and inspire in me the fire of Divine Love. Let the love flow through me to all the living.*

SHALL no longer call you servants, because a servant does not know what his master is doing. I have called you friends.

SEPT. 1

—Jn 15:15

REFLECTION. A friend is dearer to us than a million dollars.

St. John Chrysostom said, "It should be better for us that the sun were extinguished than that we should be without friends."

PRAYER. *Dear Lord, I am privileged to have You as my Friend. Thank You for this precious gift. Help me to have true friends to share my joy with, and to encourage me along the way.*

———————

 OVE the Lord, you faithful ones. The Lord looks after those who are loyal.

SEPT. 2

—Ps 31:24

REFLECTION. Loyalty is the quality of fidelity and constancy. To be loyal is to be faithful.

Pray for the grace of final perseverance, so that you will be loyal to the Lord until the very end.

PRAYER. *Jesus, my Lord and my God, help me to be Your faithful friend all the days of my life.*

129

CHEERFUL glance brings joy to the heart.

—Prov 15:30

REFLECTION. Have you ever had a person smile at you across a room? Doesn't it bring a smile to your face? It brings joy to your heart as well.

Thank God for the seasons of your life. Repay Him with your best deeds, thoughts, feelings and prayers. And be convinced that He is smiling at you from His throne in heaven.

PRAYER. *Holy Spirit of joy, I swim in the ocean of Your love.*

YOU shall call upon Me and come and pray to Me, and I will hear you.

—Jer 29:12

REFLECTION. Even when you do not know what to say in prayer the Holy Spirit will come and help you, as St. Paul states in his Letter to the Romans (8:26).

Therefore, ask the Lord to banish fear from your heart.

PRAYER. *Thank You, Most Holy Spirit. You know my needs before I even ask. All I can do is thank You again and again.*

AY the gracious care of the Lord, our God, rest upon us and prosper the works of our hands.

—Ps 90:17

SEPT.
5

REFLECTION. Early in September we celebrate Labor Day. St. Benedict once wrote, "To work is to pray."

Try to make all the acts you perform each day a little prayer of thanksgiving.

PRAYER. *O Lord, may the work of my hands and mind be pleasing to You. I offer all that I do this day as a song of gratitude. This is the song that makes me exceedingly happy.*

———

LOVE You, O Lord, my strength. The Lord is my rock, my fortress, my deliverer.

—Ps 18:2

SEPT.
6

REFLECTION. In Nehemiah 8:10 we read, "Do not be saddened, for rejoicing in the Lord is your strength."

This means that we are supposed to rejoice in the Lord's willingness to be our strength. To get the full benefit of God's participation in your life, you have to enjoy it.

PRAYER. *I will be joyful, Lord, even in times of trial and darkness. I sense Your joyful Presence deep within me. You are my untrembling center.*

131

DAILY I was the Lord's delight, rejoicing before Him always, rejoicing in His inhabited world and delighting in the human race. —Prov 8:30-31

REFLECTION. Make your entire being and life a feast of thanksgiving. Rejoice immensely and jubilantly for the gift of life. You were made for joy.

Be the miracle God intended you to be.

PRAYER. *O Lord, let me be one with You, Who are threefold holy. Grant me Your grace and Your holiness. Help me to rejoice at all times, and in all ways.*

HAIL [Mary], full of grace, the Lord is with you. —Lk 1:28

REFLECTION. Today is Mary's birthday, mine too. Jesus honors His Mother on this day.

We honor her too because she said yes to God, and became the Mother of Jesus and our mother.

PRAYER. *Dear Jesus, today we celebrate the feast of the Birth of Your Mother Mary. Help me to imitate her so that my soul may glorify the Lord and my spirit may rejoice in God my Savior.*

HERE is no treasure like a healthy body; no happiness like a joyful heart. —Sir 30:10

SEPT. 9

REFLECTION. Decide to be cheerful. Render others cheerful. Praise the whole Creation with your cheers. Be a rock against sadness, pessimism, and hopelessness.

Switch on and keep on in yourself the cheerful buttons, those marked joy, laughter, happiness, love, passion for life, gratitude for life.

–Robert Mueller

PRAYER. *Give me a grateful heart, O Lord, and I will honor You with my gladness.*

 S Jesus walked along, He saw a man who had been blind from birth. His disciples asked Him, "Rabbi, who sinned, this man or his parents, that he was born blind?" Jesus answered, "Neither this man nor his parents sinned." —Jn 9:1-3

SEPT. 10

REFLECTION. Jesus thundered His disapproval of the idea that physical disabilities are a sign of God's disfavor.

He reassured the blind man that he was not cursed, but was blessed by a loving God.

PRAYER. *Dear Jesus, thank You for bringing us the Good News that God is Unchanging Love. I rejoice in this knowledge.*

ETER came up to Him and asked, "Lord, if my brother sins against me, how often must I forgive him? As many as seven times?" Jesus answered, "I say to you, not seven times but seventy times seven." —Mt 18:21

REFLECTION. You have the power to bring your precious contribution to the happiness of the world.

Believe in the everlasting effects of your good acts, especially your willingness to forgive.

PRAYER. *Father, I want to forgive. Give me the grace to say yes I forgive once and for all. Though I cannot forget, I leave my bad feelings with You.*

 UST as the body is dead without a spirit, so faith without works is also dead. —Jas 2:26

REFLECTION. True faith is more than words. It is a kind of joyful surrender. In dying on the Cross, Jesus did more than believe in God; He obeyed Him.

He went to Jerusalem against the advice of friends because His Father asked it. Jesus knew the danger before Him, but He went anyway.

PRAYER. *Father, teach me to put my faith into action. I do not believe that my good deeds will save me, for You have done that for me, but I do believe that my charitable acts are pleasing to You.*

134

ND behold, I am with you always, to the end of the world.

—Mt 28:20

REFLECTION. The word loneliness has a certain stigma to it. People think of it as something to be ashamed of, something to hide.

In fact, the pain of loneliness is a universal problem. It is part of the human condition. Each one of us is unique. As distinct individuals, we have a built-in need to be connected. Thank God we are intimately united to Jesus forever.

PRAYER. *Dear Lord, I am connected with You at all times. Feelings are not facts. I feel lonely at times, but by faith I know You are always with me.*

ESUS said, "I am the Way, and the Truth, and the Life. No one can come to the Father except through Me."

—Jn 14:6

REFLECTION. So many times we hear people saying, "What am I to do?" or "Where should I be going with my life?"

The answer is to be found in the words of Jesus. Seek Him first and the rest will be shown to you.

PRAYER. *Lord, I do recognize You as the Way, the Truth, and the Life. Take me to the Father, today and at the hour of my death.*

GOD has given help to Israel His servant, mindful of His mercy—even as He spoke to our fathers.

—Lk 1:54-55

SEPT.
15

REFLECTION. God gives help to all who ask, as soon as they ask. Do not doubt this important truth.

That is why it is so important to call on the Lord as soon as you feel fear or start your negative thinking. Repeat the Name of Jesus often, and peace will come.

PRAYER. *Lord Jesus, come to me and remove my fears. I know You are present even when I am alone. I need to laugh at my bad feelings. Help me to trust You more.*

———

IF you abide in Me and My words abide in you, you may ask for whatever you wish, and it will be done for you. —Jn 15:7

SEPT.
16

REFLECTION. Learn to pray more and worry less. Pray, pray, pray. Pope Pius XII said: "Prayer is the key to the treasures of God. It is the weapon of combat and of victory in every battle for good over evil."

PRAYER. *Heavenly Lord, let me never forget the power of prayer. Impress it on my mind.*

WILL bring them into My holy mount, and will make them joyful in My house of prayer. —Isa 56:7

SEPT.
17

REFLECTION. The Lord wants your joyful worship—not merely in private devotions but in public prayer.

The Church is the Mystical Body of Christ at prayer. Christ lives and prays in each of us.

PRAYER. *Lord Jesus, grant me the grace to stay close to the Church all my life. Let me frequent the Sacraments and share in Your life more fully. Give me the courage to invite others to pray with me.*

 LLELUIA! Praise, all servants of the Lord, praise the Name of the Lord. —Ps 113:1

SEPT.
18

REFLECTION. How accurate we are to attribute all our blessings to the Lord. He is worthy of all our praise.

When we praise God, joy explodes from the mind and heart. With each passing day our lives become "alleluias." We become a worshiping people.

PRAYER. *Lord, You have the words of eternal life. I do love You and I praise Your Name.*

ESUS . . . , having loved His own who were in the world, loved them to the end. —Jn 13:1

SEPT. 19

REFLECTION. What a world this would be if every person meditated three minutes a day on the sentence, "God loves me!" Lives would be transformed.

We view life and its harsh realities with rose-colored glasses when we know by faith that we are loved.

PRAYER. *Lord Jesus, I hear Your words and I will act upon them by trusting You more and more. Help me to trust myself in the process.*

———————

 VERYONE who hears My words and does not act upon them will be likened to a foolish person who built a house on sand. —Mt 7:26

SEPT. 20

REFLECTION. We all must make choices on how we will act in the future.

All the Lord is saying is that we should be wise enough to think about the consequences of our actions.

PRAYER. *O Lord, grant me insight into the choices that I make, whether they be life choices or everyday decisions. Let them all be grounded in You so that they may all build up Your Kingdom.*

GOD'S love was revealed in our midst in this way: He sent His only Son . . . that we might have life through Him.

SEPT.
21

—1 Jn 4:9

REFLECTION. The Lord was made flesh—He became our brother—to save us from our pride, our disorder, our selfish selves.

He tells us that indeed we have great value, that each one of us is precious. He tells us of God's Unchanging Love. He speaks of justice, human dignity, freedom. Jesus shows the way.

PRAYER. *Dear Lord, grant that I may be an extension of Your hands, Your eyes, Your loving Heart in this troubled world. I delight in knowing that You live in me and act through me.*

LET those who suffer as Christians not be ashamed but glorify God under this name.

SEPT.
22

—1 Pet 4:16

REFLECTION. The Lord did not come to suppress suffering or deny it, but rather to fill it with His presence.

He taught us that all suffering when united with His can glorify God and save souls.

PRAYER. *Dear Lord, this is a great mystery, which I believe but do not understand fully. You chose suffering as the coin that purchased our redemption. I surrender to Your superior wisdom.*

HILE we have the opportunity, let us labor for the good of all, but especially for those members of the household of the faith. —Gal 6:10

REFLECTION. Families are individuals joined by blood or marriage, trying to love one another. The constant effort of love is difficult.

At times some members of the family have greater needs than others, making them more troublesome to live with. Don't give up on them.

PRAYER. *Dear Jesus, help me to be patient with my relatives. None of them is perfect, but then neither am I.*

 N my affliction I called upon the Lord . . . and from His temple He heard my voice. —Ps 18:7

REFLECTION. Before Archbishop Oscar Romero was martyred he wrote these precious words:

"I am obliged to give my life for those I love who are all Salvadorians, even those that are going to assassinate me. If they complete their threats, then I offer to God my blood for the redemption of El Salvador. Martyrdom is a grace from God that I do not merit. But if God accepts the sacrifice of my life, my blood must be the seed of liberty and a sign of hope that will soon be a reality . . . if they kill me, I forgive and bless those who do it."

PRAYER. *In You, O Lord, I find my strength.*

HERE your treasure is, there will your heart also be.

—Mt 6:21

REFLECTION. Christians kiss the crucifix in reverence. They hang it prominently in their homes. Respectfully, they trace the Sign of His Cross on themselves.

This religious symbol proclaims that there is no greater love in all the world. By His Death and Resurrection, Jesus has saved the world.

PRAYER. *Lord, You laid down Your life that I might live joyfully for all eternity. You are my greatest treasure.*

 APPY are the people whose God is the Lord.

—Ps 144:15

SEPT. 26

REFLECTION. Think of a cloudy day. You may not feel the sun's warmth on a cloudy day, but you know it is there hiding behind the clouds. God's love is like that.

God's love is unchanging. It is present whether you feel it or not. His love is as constant as the sun. Morning, noon or night, the sun is always shining.

PRAYER. *Lord, You are the Source of all Good. You have created us for Yourself. You are our destiny. I love You.*

OUR kindness is a greater joy than life itself.

—Ps 63:3

REFLECTION. Talking to God is like talking with a friend. A friend is one who accepts us as we are, when we are at our best or at our worst.

God is like that. He sees through the unreal image we sometimes present to others, even to ourselves. He accepts us, warts and all.

PRAYER. *Father, Son, and Holy Spirit, the Good News seems too good to be true at times. And yet I know it is true. You love me just as I am.*

 HEN he calls to Me, I will answer, and I will be with him in time of distress.

—Ps 91:15

REFLECTION. Prayer is as individual as a handprint. Kindergarten youngsters in one Milwaukee class made individual handprints as gifts for Father's Day. One little girl presented hers to her dad and said, "This is me. There's no other hand like mine in the world."

You do not have to imitate anyone else to please the Lord. Just be yourself.

PRAYER. *Dear Jesus, I am smiling in my heart. Thank You for being my secret lover.*

CHASTISED a little, they shall be greatly blessed, because God tried them and found them worthy of Himself.

SEPT.
29

—Ps 33:4

REFLECTION. I asked God for strength, / that I might achieve. / I was made weak, / that I might learn humbly to obey. . . .

I asked for health, / that I might do greater things. / I was given infirmity, / that I might do better things. . . .

I asked for all things, / that I might enjoy life. / I was given life, / that I might enjoy all things. . . .

I got nothing that I asked for— / but everything I had hoped for. / Almost despite myself, / my unspoken prayers were answered. / I am among all men, most richly blessed!

—*Excerpts from the Prayer of*
an Unknown Confederate Soldier

 LORD, You have examined me and You know me. You know when I sit and when I stand; You perceive my thoughts from a distance. You mark when I go out and when I lie down; all my ways are open to You.

SEPT.
30

—Ps 139:1-3

REFLECTION. Talking to God helps you to feel His strength in your weakness.

Do not be ashamed of the things you have done and keep on doing. Weakness can bring you closer to God.

PRAYER. *Dear Lord, I am what I am and You know me well. Thank You for Your love.*

ROOTED and grounded in love, may you be able . . . to know Christ's love, which surpasses understanding.

OCT.
1

—Eph 3:17-19

REFLECTION. The feast of St. Therese of the Child Jesus reminds us of her simple childlike faith. She once said, "Everything I have ever done, I have done to make God happy."

When you love others you enjoy pleasing them. Such was her love of God.

PRAYER. *Lord, give me the grace to be a loving child in Your Presence. Teach me how to make You happy.*

HE will give His Angels charge over you, to guard you wherever you go.

OCT.
2

—Ps 91:11

REFLECTION. How do Guardian Angels help us? St. John of the Cross had this to say about Guardian Angels: "They nourish our souls with their delightful inspirations as well as their Divine Communications."

They also give light to the mind.

PRAYER. *Heavenly Father, You send the Angels to guide and comfort us. Thank You for my Guardian Angel who teaches me that all the way to heaven is heaven.*

THERE is no fear in love. Indeed perfect love casts out fear, because fear has to do with punishment. The one who fears is not made perfect in love.

OCT. 3

—1 Jn 4:18

REFLECTION. The human heart yearns for acceptance and love.

Love drives out fear and paves the way for a joyful life.

PRAYER. *Father in heaven, bless me with wisdom enough to reject fear in all its forms as toxic and self-defeating. Lead me into the Light of Love.*

WORSHIP the Lord with gladness; enter His presence with songs of exultation.

OCT. 4

—Ps 100:2

REFLECTION. On the feast of St. Francis of Assisi we recall his appreciation of the joyful spirit in this passage:

"Do you want to know one of the best ways to win people over, and lead them to God? It consists in giving them joy and making them happy." Seize the day, and make someone a little happier.

PRAYER. *Dear Lord, St. Francis had a joyful heart, and that is probably why he is so admired throughout the world. I offer You my heart and ask You to make it joyful. Transform my sadness and my pain into joy.*

ND as Jesus prayed, the appearance **OCT.** of His countenance was changed, and His raiment became white as **5** snow. —Lk 9:29

REFLECTION. Prayer is a way of opening oneself to the splendor of Divine Life. Pure prayer is in the will to give yourself to God—just the way you are.

The Lord receives you as you are and transforms you into something luminous. All this takes time, so be patient.

PRAYER. *Dear Jesus, help me to pray as You have prayed. Give me the eyes of faith to know that You are with me always.*

UT the Advocate, the Holy Spirit, . . . **OCT.** will teach you all things and bring to mind everything I have said to you. **6** —Jn 14:26

REFLECTION. Remember to call upon the Name of the Lord as soon as you feel yourself slipping into self-pity. Think about Jesus.

Remember His words: "Be at peace . . . do not be afraid . . . have confidence . . . I am with you always."

PRAYER. *Holy Spirit, soul of my soul, You are my comfort and my strength. I thank You for loving me and holding me close.*

E proclaim Christ crucified. . . . To those who are called . . . Christ is the power of God and the wisdom of God. —1 Cor 1:23-24

OCT. 7

REFLECTION. On the feast of the Holy Rosary we remember the various scenes of Christ's life.

The Joyful Mysteries recall His Birth. The Sorrowful Mysteries remind us of His Passion and Death. The Glorious Mysteries proclaim the Resurrection, a wonderful source of joy for one and all.

PRAYER. *Lord Jesus, today is the feast of our Lady of the Rosary. May Your Holy Mother help me to pray the Rosary more often and with greater fervor.*

OW I . . . am convinced with regard to you that you yourselves are full of love. —Rom 15:14

OCT. 8

REFLECTION. Reportedly the last words of one of the world's most dedicated caregivers, Mother Teresa of Calcutta, were "I love You, Jesus."

There was no doubt in her mind about her vocation. She took Jesus' admonition literally: 'Whatever you did for one of the least of these brothers of Mine, you did for Me" (Mt 25:40).

PRAYER. *Dear Lord, thanks to You, I am full of love. It is my vocation to be a channel of Your Divine Love wherever I go, and whatever I do.*

JUST as Christ was raised from the dead through the glory of the Father, so we also may walk in newness of life.

OCT.
9

—Rom 6:4

REFLECTION. The joy of walking in the newness of life is easy for those who trust the Lord.

Whatever your weaknesses may be, turn them over to Jesus. Let Him transform you gradually into a new creation.

PRAYER. *Send Your Spirit of truth into my heart, Almighty God, so that I may remain faithful to You in my words and deeds. I need Your help in accepting my limitations while I strive to be better.*

BY charity serve one another.

OCT.
10

—Gal 5:13b

REFLECTION. Serving is not merely waiting on people. We serve others in every act of kindness and courtesy. Love begets love.

What a blessing it is to be able to give a helping hand, while being joyful in the process.

PRAYER. *Dear Jesus, make me a channel of Your love and joy. Bestow a shower of new graces upon me this day.*

OD opposes the proud, but He gives grace to the humble. Therefore, humble yourselves under the mighty hand of God, so that at the proper time He may exalt you. Cast all your anxiety on Him, because He cares deeply about you. —1 Pet 5:5-7

OCT. 11

REFLECTION. Be grateful for the gift of God's love. The fruit of appreciation is joy. A grateful heart is the sign of spiritual maturity.

PRAYER. *Dear Jesus, I am deeply grateful to know that You care for me on good days and bad. That You care deeply is amazing.*

 LL that is born of God overcomes the world; and this is the victory that overcomes the world, our faith. —1 Jn 5:4

OCT. 12

REFLECTION. Faith can move mountains. That means there are no limits to what faith can do. Think of it, no limits. You can change the world.

If you have people in your life who are making you miserable, pray for them. Change is always possible. In the Lord's good time miracles happen.

PRAYER. *Increase my faith, O Lord. Help me in my unbelief that I may have victory over my doubts and fears.*

O not be overcome by evil, but overcome evil with good.

—Rom 12:21

REFLECTION. Clara Barton, founder of the American nursing profession, never held a grudge. Once a friend reminded her of something cruel that had been done to her but she seemed not to remember it.

"Don't you remember the wrong that was done to you?" the friend asked. "No," Clara answered, "I distinctly remember forgetting that."

PRAYER. *Dear Lord, help me to let go of past hurts. I will turn them all over to You. Take care of the justice issue for me; meanwhile let me experience the joy of forgetting.*

 O not judge, and you will not be judged. Do not condemn, and you will not be condemned. Forgive, and you will be forgiven.

—Lk 6:37

REFLECTION. The spirit of forgiveness is a key element in our pursuit of happiness. Forgive others to improve your own emotional health, as well as to please the Lord.

To live well it is necessary to strive for a forgiving heart.

PRAYER. *Lord, I forgive; help me in my unforgiveness. The memories are painful, but I turn them all over to You.*

ESUS said, "If anyone loves Me, he will keep My words, and My Father will love him, and We will come to him.

—Jn 14:23

REFLECTION. It must be stressed over and over again that the Lord actually comes into you. He permeates, pervades, and penetrates every cell in your body.

You do not have to feel it emotionally—you simply have to know it as a matter of faith. The Kingdom of God is within.

PRAYER. *Father, Son, and Holy Spirit, Indwelling Trinity, I am Yours today and always.*

F you forgive other for the wrongs they have done, your heavenly Father will also forgive you.

—Mt 6:14

REFLECTION. Think about being forgiven for the greatest wrong you have ever done. Doesn't that feel great?

It is in your power to give this gift to someone else. Forgiveness is a precious gift. Why not give it? So what if it is not appreciated. You will be the bigger person. You will be doing the Lord's Will.

PRAYER. *Lord God, I have sinned. I know Your Mercy is simply another name for Your Love. Thank You for washing away my sins.*

DEATH is swallowed up in victory. O death, where is your victory? O death, where is your sting?

—1 Cor 15:54-55

17

REFLECTION. In a world that denies death and does everything to hide it, it is urgently necessary to recall the inevitability of an event that is part of the history of every person.

— *Pope John Paul II*

PRAYER. *Lord, help me to meditate upon my own death. Let me do so not in a morbid fascination, but rather in recognition that in death I come home to You.*

RECEIVE the Word, which has been planted in you and can save you.

—Jas 1:21

OCT.

18

REFLECTION. The Word of God is wisdom. The gift of wisdom is often called the most beneficial gift of the Holy Spirit because it opens us to a wonderful new level of holiness and happiness.

It is said that where your treasure is, there your heart will be also. That is true because your treasure is where you give most of your attention.

PRAYER. *Come, Holy Spirit, fill me with Your knowledge and wisdom that I may serve You joyfully and loyally all the days of my life.*

152

HERE is one God, and there is one Mediator between God and man, Christ Jesus, Himself a Man, Who gave Himself as a ransom for all. —1 Tim 2:5

OCT. 19

REFLECTION. Here is what St. Augustine wrote about how to find joy in God:

"I sought for a way of gaining strength sufficient to have joy in You [God] but I did not find it, until I embraced the Mediator between God and man, the Man Jesus Christ, Who is over all things, God blessed forever."

PRAYER. *Dear Jesus, I believe that You are indeed the Way, the answer to all my needs. I put my trust in You and I love You with all my heart.*

LL of God's creatures differ . . . , yet none of them has He made in vain. For each is good. Can one ever see enough of their splendor? —Sir 42:25

OCT. 20

REFLECTION. A real Christian is color blind when it comes to race.

Pope John Paul II said: "Love responds generously to the needs of the poor, and it is marked by compassion for those in sorrow."

PRAYER. *O Lord the Saints reached out in a truly heroic manner to those who were of a different race and religion. May my love be just as fruitful and just as color blind.*

153

ILL not God grant justice to His elect who cry out to Him day and night? Will He delay in answering their pleas? I tell you, He will grant them justice quickly.

—Lk 18:7-8

REFLECTION. If you feel lonely, turn to Jesus more and more. Ignore your bad feelings. Laugh at them. But be prepared to take some positive action. Get involved. Become a volunteer.

Loneliness is an illusion for those who believe.

PRAYER. *Thank You, Lord, for this word. In all circumstances, I give thanks to You, my Lord and God, for Your protection and care. Keep me ever at Your side.*

 OMAN, you have great faith. Let it be done for you as you wish.

—Mt 15:28

REFLECTION. There are times when we must pass through a dark valley. We feel as though God has abandoned us.

Do not believe it. He is right there wondering if we trust Him enough to be brave. It pleases Him immensely when we whistle in the dark.

PRAYER. *Thank You, Jesus. Increase my confidence in You. Help me to understand that my peace will be found in Your Will and that the crosses of my life are opportunities for growth. Protect me from my fears.*

E died for all, so that those who live might no longer live for themselves, but for Him Who for their sake died and was raised to life. —2 Cor 5:15

OCT. **23**

REFLECTION. In His sacrifice we begin to penetrate the mystery of spiritual joy.

Jesus on the very night before His Passion and Death said, "I have revealed these things to you so that My joy may be in you and your joy may be complete" (Jn 15:11).

PRAYER. *Jesus, help me to grow deeper in my understanding of this truth. By dying to myself, I will find the gateway to a greater immersion in Your life of joy and peace.*

OUR Word is a lamp for my feet and a light to my path. —Ps 119:105

OCT. **24**

REFLECTION. Once again we proclaim the Lord as a guiding light.

Do you know what it is to walk with a flashlight in the night? All around you is darkness, but your step is safe. You see the rocks and pitfalls. The word of God is like that. It guides your steps.

PRAYER. *Jesus, You are my Light and my Companion. In this dangerous world I am not left in the dark. Thank You.*

155

DO not concern myself with great affairs or with things too sublime for me. Rather, I have stilled and calmed my soul.

OCT.
25

—Ps 131:1-2

REFLECTION. Learn to calm your soul. The art of happiness involves a certain amount of self-discipline.

Reject negative thoughts, and the toxic emotions that follow them will gradually clear up and dissipate. Learn to quiet your mind and spirit.

PRAYER. *Jesus, help me to be still and not be afraid because You are always there, loving me, and giving me strength.*

 WILL hear what the Lord God says: truly He speaks of peace to His people

OCT.
26

—Ps 85:9

REFLECTION. In order to hear you must learn to listen. To listen is to give full attention to the one speaking.

Let the words of the Scriptures enter your heart. Like the yeast in a loaf of freshly baked bread, you will be lifted up.

PRAYER. *Come to me, my Lord and my God, and fill me with Your wisdom and light. Fill me with Your joy that my spirit may miraculously rise.*

156

E leads me to tranquil streams. He restores my soul.

—Ps 23:1

REFLECTION. The Lord will indeed lead you and calm your soul. This truth is at the heart of every authentic religious experience.

The Holy Spirit always leads us in directions we would not have chosen for ourselves. Why is that? Because He leads us in the direction of love, and wherever there is love, there is joy.

PRAYER. *Holy Spirit of Love, I live in You, and I draw strength from You. Help me to reflect more on the reality of Your Presence in my soul.*

OR as the heavens are exalted above the earth, so are My ways exalted above your ways.

—Isa 55:9

REFLECTION. Believing in supernatural mysteries is a sign of wisdom. Many call it foolishness, but they are in the dark.

We can never fully understand God's ways, but we can come to a deeper sense of reverence for them.

PRAYER. *Father, give me the wisdom of Job. In the face of so much suffering He continually gave You the benefit of the doubt. He kept saying, "God gives and God takes away. Blessed be God." I want to make that my prayer too.*

ET us consider how to spur one another to love and good works.

—Heb 10:24

REFLECTION. We do not fully appreciate the impact a kind or encouraging word can have on someone. Think about it.

Always have a plan in mind when you are in contact with someone. How can I spur this person on to greatness?

PRAYER. *O Lord, the only plan I have is in trusting You to show me the way, one day at a time. Give me the urge to help my neighbor, especially when I am feeling selfish and lazy.*

———————

EHOLD what manner of love the Father has bestowed upon us, that we should be called children of God.

—1 Jn 3:1

REFLECTION. Imagine being the child of a great king. That would make you a member of the royal family.

The next time you look in the mirror, try saying it out loud: I am a princess (prince). I am chosen to live in the royal palace.

PRAYER. *I am smiling, Lord. I feel a long way from the royal palace, but it certainly is nice to know that one day it will be so. One day I will be with You in paradise.*

FINALLY, find your strength in the Lord and in His mighty power.

OCT.
31

—Eph 6:10

REFLECTION. If you want to be strong begin by being thankful in all circumstances. Start everyday with an overflowing heart full of thanks.

Thank God for every moment of your life. Never complain or be bitter. Reject every form of self-pity.

PRAYER. *Jesus, when I am grateful then I am strong. My gratitude banishes the bad feelings that weigh me down. When I feel Your gratitude to the Father pulsing through me, I am strong in Your strength. Thank You, Lord.*

ALL these people gave their gifts to God out of their wealth. But [this widow] out of her poverty gave all that she had to live on.

NOV.
1

—Lk 21:4

REFLECTION. All Saints Day reminds us that living a holy life means that we must strive to be saintly. It also reminds us of the heroes who have gone before us.

Always remember that you are a Saint in training, a good person trying to be better.

PRAYER. *O Lord, help me to practice the art of love more diligently. Give me a heart of charity for the most neglected among us.*

ALL who love Me, I also love. And those who seek Me find Me.

—Prov 8:17

REFLECTION. St. Thomas Aquinas once wrote, "The worst day in purgatory will be better than the best day we ever spent on earth."

Isn't that an amazing statement? Think about it. Those in purgatory are in the dressing room, preparing for the banquet. We on earth are not finished with the testing period.

PRAYER. *O Lord, I pray for all my deceased loved ones. Eternal rest grant to them and let perpetual light shine upon them. They are better off than I, so I am not really worried, but I do hope I will join them one day in the splendor of heaven.*

AS for me, I trust in Your kindness; my heart rejoices in Your salvation. I will sing to the Lord because He has been good to me.

—Ps 13:6-7

REFLECTION. The Lord is delighted with us when we delight in Him.

Have hope. Lift up your heart and have a new confidence.

God is your shield in times of trouble. Why should you be afraid?

PRAYER. *Jesus, my Lord and my God, make my heart like unto Yours.*

WILL close their wounds and give them **NOV.** health . . . and I will reveal to them the prayer of peace. —Jer 33:6 **4**

REFLECTION. For those who do not believe in Divine Providence, no argument will be sufficient to convince them to trust God. For those who do believe, no explanation is necessary.

Believe! Become a beautiful instrument of God's healing love.

PRAYER. *Lord, make me an instrument of Your peace. Where there is hatred, let me sow love, where there is injury, pardon, and where there is sadness, joy.*

 E shepherds of the flock of God that has **NOV.** been entrusted to your care. . . . Do not lord it over those in your charge, but be **5** examples to the flock. —1 Pet 5:2-3

REFLECTION. We lead by good example. Those in authority must lead by good example, and they must also pray for the wisdom to govern and teach with skill and compassion.

Christianity means putting God first, neighbor second, and self third.

PRAYER. *Dear Jesus, protect and guide those in authority, and do the same for me. May I learn to be courageous in setting a good example for my neighbor.*

E said to them, "Go you also and work in My vineyard, and I will give you whatever is just."

—Mt 20:4

REFLECTION. Do not be afraid of exerting yourself for the Lord. A little work for the spiritual well-being of your neighbor can go a long way.

Keep in mind the wonderful heavenly retirement program when you extend yourself for others.

PRAYER. *Dear Jesus, I will follow You and work in Your vineyard with trust and patience. Just give me the will to be charitable and the grace to persevere.*

Y trust is in You, O Lord. I say, "You are my God." My destiny is in Your hands.

—Ps 31:15-16

REFLECTION. What a pleasure it is to be able to say, in all honesty, "My trust is in You, O Lord."

The person who can say that is relieved of the enormous burden of fear.

PRAYER. *Lord, I do say it. I do trust You. At times I become a little unsettled, but so did John the Baptist whom You called the greatest person born of woman. So I am not alone in this feeling. I know You understand.*

162

HEAL the sick. . . . Freely you have received; freely give.

—Mt 10:8

REFLECTION. There are many subtle ways to heal a person. A troubled heart can be soothed by a kind phone call or a caring letter. Your efforts can lift up a downcast spirit and bring a smile.

You see, you can be a healer right now, and you do not even know it.

PRAYER. *Lord, give me the prompting I need to write that letter or make that call. I know plenty of people who could use some cheer in their lives.*

BLESSED are the people who know You, O Lord, who walk in the light of Your countenance.

—Ps 89:16

REFLECTION. You have the power to bring a smile to the face of someone close to you. A cheerful person is a delight for everyone.

Decide to be a person who builds up rather than tears down. Walking in the light can do wonders for the state of your happiness.

PRAYER. *Jesus, I walk in Your Light. I feel Your smile upon me, and like an infant in a crib, I return the smile wholeheartedly.*

VERY good tree bears good fruit.
—Mt 7:17

REFLECTION. You are a good tree if you follow Jesus and build your life on His promises. That means whether you understand it or not, you will produce good fruit with your life.

Receive the power of the Sacraments, and follow your inner light. The Lord will lead you.

PRAYER. *Jesus, You are the Light of my life. Feed me and lead me. I am Yours.*

MEN, I say to you, unless you change and become like little children, you will never enter the Kingdom of Heaven. —Mt 18:3

REFLECTION. A child is one who trusts. Survival depends on it.

The most important work is not that which you do: it is that which you allow the Lord to do through you. Trust Him.

Do not worry about the results of your work the Lord will give it growth and fruitfulness in the measure in which it is entrusted to Him.

The more you give, the more He will increase your capacity for growing.

PRAYER. *Lord, bestow on me the grace to be childlike in my love for You. I trust You and I will follow You all the days of my life.*

F you are willing to obey, you will eat the **NOV.** best food the land has to offer.

—Isa 1:19

12

REFLECTION. The spiritual life of a person does not consist of mere attention to one's soul, but of a free and unconditional response to the call of the Holy Spirit, whatever the cost may be. . . .

It is a life soaked through and through by a sense of His reality and claim. Christ's whole ministry was an illustration of this mystery.

—Evelyn Underhill

PRAYER. *Dear Holy Spirit, Soul of my soul, I am listening. I want You to be the center of my life. I am Yours.*

 F you love those who love you, what re- **NOV.** ward will you get?

—Mt 5:46

13

REFLECTION. This is the hardest thing to understand. We are actually expected to love people who do not care a twit for us. Do you see why? The Lord loves them, but they do not know it. He is depending on you to be His channel of communications.

You do not need words. Just do a kind deed now and then; even a smile can open the door to a new beginning for someone in need.

PRAYER. *Extend my love, O Lord, beyond my family and friends to those who need my concern. Let me reach out to them in concrete ways.*

YOU have been called to freedom, brothers and sisters; only do not use freedom as an occasion for sensuality.

—Gal 5:13a

REFLECTION. Feel free, you are not bound by servile fear. Genuine love is the supreme law. That means you have to be free from public opinion so that you may love those in need. Even if your peers think you are crazy for taking the risk, do it anyway.

Remember, the overweight lady is Christ, so is the prisoner, and the alcoholic. The Lord comes into our lives in various disguises.

PRAYER. *Heavenly Father, teach me to cherish the freedom that is Your gift, a freedom that is not afraid to commit itself to love.*

LEAVING the Sanhedrin, the Apostles rejoiced that they had been found worthy to suffer disgrace for the sake of the Name.

—Acts 5:41

REFLECTION. Feeling joy while one is suffering public disgrace for the Lord may seem a contradiction, but the Saints experienced it all the time. This joy is a by-product of surrendering to the Lord.

"Blessed are you when you are persecuted for My sake" (Mt 5:11). These words are true.

PRAYER. *Dear Lord, the Gospel message often baffles me. Help me to understand these supernatural truths, and more importantly, help me to trust You completely.*

RAY for those who persecute you.
—Mt 5:44

REFLECTION. If you are going to have real joy in your heart and soul you must be willing to forgive. The best way to forgive is to pray for that person.

No family can live in harmony without repeated acts of forgiveness. However, you do not have to become a doormat for anyone.

PRAYER. *Father, I forgive, but I need help with my bad feelings. I know that in time those feelings will evaporate as long as the offending party changes.*

 FTER hearing the Word of God, they hold it fast with a right and good heart and bear fruit in patience.
—Lk 8:15

REFLECTION. Let a person come forward, a living person capable of speaking to the heart; let truth flow from this person's life and let the person's power be matched by an equal gift of love.

Then people will listen to the Good News, and the dawn of better days will brighten our skies. —*Cardinal Duval (pastoral letter)*

PRAYER. *Dear Jesus, I have heard Your Word and I come forward to follow You. Let me speak the truth with hope, and together we will bear rich fruit.*

B Y faith their weakness was turned into strength as they became mighty in battle and put foreign armies to flight.

NOV. 18

—Heb 11:33-34

REFLECTION. The Lord is waiting for your trust. You can give Him your weakness, your problems, your weariness.

He is ready to make His power available. You have only to ask.

PRAYER. *Lord, help me to understand Your silence the way St. Paul did. It is a silence that gives power to those who have faith.*

A MEN, I say to you, whatever you did for one of the least of these brothers of Mine, you did for Me.

NOV. 19

—Mt 25:40

REFLECTION. This text is the most important one in all the Scriptures.

Once you understand it, your life will never be the same.

Jesus continues to live His passion. He continues to fall, poor and hungry, just as He did on the way to Calvary.

PRAYER. *Lord, I have been given so much. Give me ears to hear the cry of the poor, and the will to respond generously and compassionately to You, living in them.*

IF you then, despite your evil nature, know how to give good gifts to your children, how much more will your Father in heaven give good things to those who ask Him.

NOV. 20

—Mt 7:11

REFLECTION. Try to get into the spirit of faith. Do not expect bad things to happen.

Await the Lord's goodness like a joyful child standing before the Christmas tree, awaiting the opening of the presents.

PRAYER. *I trust You, Lord, and that means I trust Your love. I can expect the best from You. Even in times of suffering I will not succumb to doubt.*

HOLY, holy, holy is the Lord of hosts! . . . All the earth is full of His glory.

NOV. 21

—Isa 6:3

REFLECTION. Take time to THINK—it is the Source of Power. / Take time to PLAY—it is the Secret of Perpetual Youth. / Take time to READ—it is the Fountain of Wisdom. / Take time to WORSHIP—it is the Highway to Reverence. / Take time to be FRIENDLY—it is the Road to Happiness. / Take time to LAUGH—it is the Music of the Soul.

PRAYER. *Lord, I want to laugh more. Teach me to laugh at myself more, especially when I am clumsy, forgetful, or just plain sinful.*

IF we have died with Christ, we believe that we shall also live with Him.

—Rom 6:8

REFLECTION. True disciples willingly accept their share of the Passion of Christ.

For without a common fate with the Lord, there is no common life with Him. Think about that.

PRAYER. *Lord, give me the strength to endure the sufferings that I must endure. Let me bear my cross without complaint. Teach me to unite my pain with Your Passion.*

 WHERE two or three are gathered together in My Name, I am there in the midst of them.

—Mt 18:20

REFLECTION. Dorothy Day of Catholic Worker fame once took a homeless woman into her shelter when it was exceedingly overcrowded.

Dorothy said, "It's all right, let her in, she can sleep with me." She was quickly warned, "Can't you see that woman is in the last stages of syphilis?" Without hesitation, Dorothy replied, "That is not a woman with syphilis; for me she is Jesus Christ."

PRAYER. *Lord, make my heart brave enough to see Your face in the least among us, and strong enough to respond in a loving way.*

170

IVE as children of light, for light produces all goodness and righteousness and truth.
—Eph 5:8-9

REFLECTION. Those who deem themselves to be Christian must be aware of the following obligation that is theirs.

They are bound by conscience to the basic, imperative duty of bearing witness to the truth in which they believe and to the grace that has transformed their soul.

—*Pope John XXIII*

PRAYER. *O Lord, teach me to make my life ever more transparent and consistent, so that I may live ever more joyfully in Your truth.*

ET my prayer rise like incense before You; the lifting of my hands, like the evening sacrifice.
—Ps 141:2

REFLECTION. Prayer is not a stratagem for occasional use, a refuge to resort to now and then. It is rather like an established residence for the innermost self. All things have a home; the bird has a nest, the fox has a hole, the bee has a hive. *A soul without prayer is a soul without a home. . . .*

To pray is to open a door where God may enter.
—*Rabbi Abraham Heschel*

PRAYER. *Blessed are You, Lord, God of my life. I bow before You and open my heart to You this day.*

YES, when you seek Me with all your heart, you will find Me with you, says the Lord. —Jer 29:13

REFLECTION. For five minutes a day quiet your imagination, close your eyes to the things of the senses, and enter within your soul, which is the temple of the Holy Spirit.

There, speak to this Divine Spirit.

PRAYER. *O Holy Spirit, soul of my soul . . . guide me, strengthen me, console me, tell me what to do. . . . I promise to submit to whatever You desire of me and to accept everything You allow to happen to me. Let me only know Your Will.* —*Cardinal Mercier*

PROCLAIM this message: "The Kingdom of Heaven is near." —Mt 10:7

REFLECTION. *Love, pray, go, teach*—these are the words of Jesus. He gives us a new view of reality, and we try to respond in a spirit of love.

God's love is the Good News of the Gospel. But there are anti-Gospel forces in the world. The evil one sows seeds of unrest, seeds of hatred. The Christ-bearer is aware of the enemy at all times, but goes forth without fear.

PRAYER. *Lord Jesus, enable me to enjoy the simple things that are so easy to take for granted, so that I may proclaim the Gospel joyfully.*

I CAME to you in weakness, in fear, and in great trepidation.

—1 Cor 2:3

NOV. 28

REFLECTION. Oliver was brain-damaged from birth: blind, mute, and paralyzed. He lived until a month before his 33rd birthday. I had the honor of preaching at his funeral.

There is much that I have learned from Oliver's meekness and poverty. He never owned anything. In a world where money and possessions are regarded as the only real security, Oliver's life gave testimony to the truth that we really live by love. He was hand-fed every spoonful of food he ever ate.

PRAYER. *Lord, help me to see Your presence in the little ones of this world.*

THROUGH Him you are believers in God, Who raised Him up . . . so that your faith and hope might be in God.

—1 Pet 1:21

NOV. 29

REFLECTION. Place your hope in God and everything else will fall in place.

All your happiness will be major and all your unhappiness will be minor. Do not try to understand it, just believe.

PRAYER. *Lord, where there is life there is hope. I am alive, and I look to You as my supreme hope. Thank You for filling me with faith and joy.*

E know that God makes all things work together for good for those who love Him. **NOV. 30**

—Rom 8:28

REFLECTION. The Lord God knows all things. He knows what you really need, not merely what you think you need. Trust Him to take care of you in His own way. It may hurt from time to time, but He knows what He is doing.

PRAYER. *Lord, I turn over my needs and my very self to You. I never seem to do it completely so I am not sure if You think I am sincere or not. But I want to be. I give myself to You warts and all, and hope that You will receive me kindly and take care of me and those I love.*

AN a mother forget her infant . . . ? Even if she should forget, I will never forget you. **DEC. 1**

—Isa 49:15

REFLECTION. Comparing God's love to a mother's love for her child helps us understand the mystery of Christmas. We anticipate the celebration of the birth of Jesus with gladness.

Advent is the season of subdued but joyful expectation. God's great tenderness is revealed in Jesus and we are filled with hope.

PRAYER. *O Lord, the Prophet told us that even if a mother were to forget her child, You would never forget us. May I ever experience that maternal love with which You love Your beloved children.*

I KEEP the Lord always before me, for with Him at my right hand I will never fall. Therefore, my heart is glad and my soul rejoices; my body too is filled with confidence. —Ps 16:8-9

DEC. 2

REFLECTION. To be close to the Lord by means of faith is to realize that feelings do not matter. By faith we know that He is always present, loving us, whether we feel it or not.

Bless the Lord on good days and bad. When troubles come, search for reasons to give thanks, for this is what the Saints before you did.

PRAYER. *Dear God, I have it in my heart to give thanks to You in all circumstances. Let me have the strength and courage to carry out these good intentions.*

 IN an acceptable time I have heard you. Behold, now is the acceptable time; behold, now is the day of salvation! —2 Cor 6:2

DEC. 3

REFLECTION. Living in the present moment means that we turn over the sins and sorrows of the past to God's mercy, and we entrust all our worries about the future to God's Divine Providence. In this way, we do not foul up the present moment with feelings of fear and self-pity.

Laugh at your fears, and carry on with joy.

PRAYER. *Dear Lord, I rejoice in the coming of the Kingdom. The day of salvation is here. Thank You for Your mercy. Thank You for Your Divine Providence.*

175

ECAUSE of the tender mercy of our God . . . the dawn from on high will break upon us to shine on those who sit in darkness and in the shadow of death, to guide our feet along the path of peace.

DEC. 4

—Lk 1:78-79

REFLECTION. Those who are united to Christ are living in the Light. They are protected and shored up by His strength.

On the other hand, how heavy the burden of life is when it is carried without Christ.

PRAYER. *Holy Spirit, I turn today's troubles over to You. Please carry them for me. Help me to toss out all my needless worries, for You are my joy and my strength.*

 HE Lord is good to all, showing compassion to every creature.

DEC. 5

—Ps 145:9

REFLECTION. All of us will be judged one day, not so much on what we dreamed, as on what we did. Even then it is not so much on what we did, but on how much love we put into the doing.

No matter what our shortcomings may be, we still will be facing a merciful Judge. The Lord has great compassion on us all. Be at peace.

PRAYER. *Father, teach me how to put my good intentions into action. In other words, teach me how to love.*

176

PEACE I leave with you, My peace I give to you. Not as the world gives do I give it to you. Do not let your hearts be troubled.
—Jn 14:27

REFLECTION. Loneliness can be a big obstacle to peace of mind. But it can also be a spur for us to become more creative.

Once we accept the fact that we will always have a certain amount of loneliness in our lives, we can live with it, and stop looking for false solutions. God is the only One Who will ultimately fill that void.

PRAYER. *Dear Jesus, You offer me Your peace, and I accept it. I also accept my loneliness as a reminder that I am never really alone, for You are with me always.*

MAY the Father grant you to be strengthened with power through His Spirit . . . and to have Christ dwelling in you through faith.
—Eph 3:16-17

REFLECTION. St. Paul prays that you will be strengthened with the power of the Holy Spirit. His prayers for you are ongoing.

You will be made strong. The fear and timidity you once knew are receding. You will be given courage and fortitude to cope with life and all its problems. Believe it.

PRAYER. *Jesus, in You I live and breathe and have my being. Let me enjoy Your company.*

THE Kingdom of God is close at hand.
—Mt 1:15

REFLECTION. Today is the great feast of the Immaculate Conception. Mary was conceived in a state of perfect purity. This event signals the beginning of God's magnificent plan to make all things new.

In this mystery, we see how well God plans ahead. He is already planning your entry into heaven.

PRAYER. *Mary conceived without sin, pray for us who have recourse to you. We pray for those most in need of God's mercy.*

THE fear of the Lord is the beginning of Wisdom.
—Prov 1:7

REFLECTION. Everyone who has suffered from scrupulosity knows that an excessive fear of God's judgment can have devastating effects on one's emotional life. Scruples are more related to one's nervous symptoms than to morality.

God is not offended by trifles. When you make a sensible effort to be good, God is pleased. Perfectionism is not Christianity.

PRAYER. *Father, help me to trust in Your mercy. I know You love me.*

JESUS came and proclaimed peace to you who were far off and peace to those who were near.

DEC. 10

—Eph 2:17

REFLECTION. Peace is offered to those close to God and those far away. He loves all His children even those who do not love Him.

Let the Lord into your heart and relax in His love. The gift of peace is the fruit of obedience to God's law of love.

PRAYER. *Lord, I do welcome You. I bathe in the wonder of Your loving presence. I am at peace.*

WHATEVER you do in word or in work, do all in the Name of the Lord Jesus, giving thanks to God the Father through Him. —Col 3:17

DEC. 11

REFLECTION. The Jesuits put these letters A.M.D.G. on everything they write. They stand for the Latin words *Ad Maiorem Dei Gloriam*, which mean "All is offered for the greater glory of God."

In this spirit, everything they do or say is offered in humble gratitude.

PRAYER. *Lord, I commit myself this day to make the world a better, happier place and to give You greater glory.*

HOW wonderful and delightful it is for people to live together in unity. . . . For there the Lord has bestowed His blessing, life forevermore. —Ps 133:1-3

DEC. 12

REFLECTION. When a family is full of love, it is a sign of the presence of the Holy Spirit.

Every member of the family should cooperate in creating an atmosphere of emotional comfort for all concerned.

PRAYER. *Lord, help me to do my share in making my home more peaceful and loving, and do not let me be too hard on myself. If others disrupt the peace, this is a heavy cross, and I need Your help to carry it.*

FOr the Father Himself loves you because you have loved Me and have believed that I came forth from God. —Jn 16:27

DEC. 13

REFLECTION. Faith in Jesus is at the heart of all spiritual progress. Jesus teaches us that God is gentle, God is kind.

When we finally grasp the simplicity of this mystery, it changes our whole outlook.

PRAYER. *Lord Jesus, send the fire of Your love into my heart to purify it. Let that fire blaze, giving light to those lost in darkness and heat to those who suffer from the cold of loneliness.*

180

OD so loved the world that He gave His only-begotten Son, so that everyone who believes in Him may not perish but attain eternal life. **DEC. 14**

—Jn 3:16

REFLECTION. Say yes to life, cheerfully enthusiastically, ecstatically.

Believe in the immortality and everlasting effects of your goodness. —*Robert Mueller*

PRAYER. *Assist me, dear Lord, in understanding the great mystery of Your love.*

 HEY shall know that I, the Lord, am their God. —Ezek 34:30 **DEC. 15**

REFLECTION. He was born in an obscure village / the child of a peasant woman. / He grew up in still another village, / where He worked in a carpenter shop / until He was thirty. / Then for three years / He was an itinerant preacher. / He never wrote a book. / He never held an office. . . . / He was nailed to a Cross / between two thieves. / While He was dying, / His executioners gambled for His clothing, / the only property He had on earth. / When He was dead, / He was laid in a borrowed grave / through the pity of a friend. / Nineteen centuries have come and gone, / and today He is the central figure / of the human race. —*One Solitary Life*

PRAYER. *Jesus, Your life is an inspiration to me. I bow before You as I await Your coming at Christmas.*

YOU have received a Spirit of adoption as children, by virtue of which we cry "Abba!" "Father!"

DEC. 16

—Rom 8:16

REFLECTION. Try to appreciate what it means to be adopted into the royal family. The Father loves you as He loves His own Son, the Second Person of the Blessed Trinity. Impossible to imagine, yes, but true nevertheless.

Hold on to this wonderful truth. The Lord played you a tune and you must dance.

PRAYER. *Lord, the knowledge of Your love boggles the mind. I am not perfect, but You love me anyway. Amazing. Yes, I will dance before You with gladness.*

 WHEN you have done everything that was commanded you, say "We are unprofitable servants."

DEC. 17

—Lk 18:10

REFLECTION. Remember that even though you are special in God's eyes, you are still a vessel of clay.

Stay bowed down in gratitude. Do not become boastful. The Lord loves a humble child.

PRAYER. *Lord, I say gladly and with full knowledge: I am Your unprofitable servant. Everything I have ever done that is good has come about by means of Your grace. Thank You for all Your gifts.*

HEN said I, "Behold, I come . . . to do Your Will, O God."
—Heb 10:7

DEC. 18

REFLECTION. As we approach Christmas, we ponder the childlike simplicity of Mary, the Mother of Jesus. Her perfect act of surrender is a model for all Christians. Mary said "Be it done unto me according to your word." Her "Yes" given to God was total, and we are called to do the same.

PRAYER. *Hail Mary, full of grace, the Lord is with you, blessed are you among women, and blessed is the fruit of your womb, Jesus.*

OME of the seeds fell into good soil, and when they grew they produced a crop of a hundredfold.
—Lk 8:8

DEC. 19

REFLECTION. Jesus tells of the seeds falling on good soil. The parable refers to the Word of God falling on the open heart of a good listener.

When that happens, there is abundant growth, a rich harvest of wisdom, charity, and joy.

PRAYER. *Holy Spirit, spread Your spiritual seeds upon me and give me life so that my charity and joy may be full.*

183

H E said to me, "My grace is sufficient for you, for strength is made perfect in weakness."

DEC.
20

—2 Cor 12:9

REFLECTION. The weaker you know yourself to be, the better off you are spiritually, according to St. Paul.

At moments of weakness and dejection, he remembered to call on the Lord for strength, and the Lord always came through to help him.

PRAYER. *Lord Jesus, I pray with confidence that You will always be there for me. You are my strength and my joy even when I feel weak and diminished.*

———

T HE time is fulfilled, and the Kingdom of God is at hand. Repent and believe in the Gospel.

DEC.
21

—Mk 1:15

REFLECTION. God is Unchanging Love. This is the most important truth to cling to as a basis for all future growth in the Lord. You are called to teach others by your words and deeds.

By believing in Him, you have His light within you. Let it shine.

PRAYER. *Father in heaven, I do not feel Your light passing through me at any given moment, but I trust that it does. I repent of ever having offended You. At the same time, I realize that You delight in using me as Your instrument.*

OD brought us to life together with Christ . . . and seated us together in heaven in Christ.

DEC. 22

—Eph 2:5-6

REFLECTION. Faith and life—these are nothing less than the realities in which we are immersed, and they are the goals to which we would draw attention.

Keep them particularly in mind during the coming happy occasion. —*Pope Paul VI*

PRAYER. *O Lord, the celebration of Christmas draws near. Help me to view this feast in the perspective of my faith. Let me celebrate with joy.*

 OSEPH went from Nazareth into Judea . . . to register together with Mary his espoused wife, who was with child.

DEC. 23

—L:k 2:4-5

REFLECTION. Joseph is rarely mentioned in the Gospels, but here we see him as the protector of Mary and the Child in her womb.

He was obedient to God and to the laws of the land, but most of all he was a comfort and support to Mary.

PRAYER. *Holy Spirit, Your love filled St. Joseph with strength and compassion. May I take the same courage and tenderness from You so that I may be a comfort to those who need me.*

HEN the fullness of time arrived, God sent His Son, born of a woman, . . . that He might redeem those under the Law. —Gal 4:4-5 **DEC. 24**

REFLECTION. Mary traveled a long distance to reach her fulfillment. All the while she kept these things hidden in her heart.

Her humility is a marvel to behold. In a spirit of humble gratitude she brought forth the Divine Infant, Jesus.

PRAYER. *O come let us adore Him; O come let us adore Him; O come let us adore Him; Christ, the Lord.*

 ARY'S days to be delivered were fulfilled, and she brought forth her firstborn Son. —Lk 2:6-7 **DEC. 25**

REFLECTION. Look upon the Baby born in Bethlehem Who is beside His Mother Mary.

Draw near to Him, prostrate yourselves to adore Him, and offer Him the gifts that you bear in your heart.

—*Pope John Paul II*

PRAYER. *My Infant Lord, I bow before You with the shepherds, the wise men, and the legions of Christians who have adored You down through the ages. Give me the best gift possible, the full knowledge of Your love.*

HE wrapped Him in swaddling clothes and laid Him in a manger, because there was no room for them in the inn. —Lk 2:7

DEC. 26

REFLECTION. Jesus is the joy of the earth; He is the physician of every human infirmity. He is personified in every person who suffers, arousing compassion and generous love.

Jesus, therefore, is present always and everywhere. —*Pope Paul VI*

PRAYER. *Come, Lord Jesus. Help me to recognize Your Presence in my life, especially in my pain. Help me to know that You have joined Your sufferings to mine, so that I may join my suffering to Yours.*

 OR a Child has been born to us, a Son has been given to us. Upon His shoulders dominion rests, and this is the Name He has been given: Wonderful Counselor, Mighty God, Eternal Father, Prince of Peace. —Isa 9:5

DEC. 27

REFLECTION. To look upon the Infant Jesus, and know that He was a Divine King, must have been an awesome experience for the shepherds.

It still is for us today. Whoever sees this Little Child, sees the One Who sent Him.

PRAYER. *There are no words in such matters. We become still and know that we are in the presence of God. Lord, I bow before You.*

REJOICE insofar as you are partakers of the sufferings of Christ, that you may also rejoice with exultation in the revelation of His glory. —1 Pet 4:13

DEC. 28

REFLECTION. Decide to be happy in Christ's love. Pope John Paul II said:

"True, you cannot always be healthy or successful, but you can always be with Christ and find strength at His side."

PRAYER. *O Lord, give me perspective during the trials of my life, and humility during my successes. Fill me with Your Spirit of joy both in good times and in bad, for You are my only true joy.*

WE have heard of your faith in Christ Jesus and of the love you bear toward all the holy ones. —Col 1:4

DEC. 29

REFLECTION. Would it not be beautiful if Christmas were to generate the inner Christ within us: a habit of meditation, a living memory of the great Mystery that we have solemnly commemorated; a persuasion of faith, now acquired and confirmed?

We must live our lives in union with Christ's life. —*Pope Paul VI*

PRAYER. *O Lord, with You at my side I am never alone. How happy that makes me feel. Thank You for Your love.*

THE wolf and the lamb will feed together. . . . They will neither harm nor destroy on My holy mountain.

—Isa 65:25

DEC. 30

REFLECTION. The peaceable Kingdom has already begun in your soul. Share this gift with those who are lost and lonely.

Let them see that you are living in the peace and joy of Christ's life.

PRAYER. *Lord, grant that I may be a genuine carrier of Your love and mercy. It fills me with an inner happiness just knowing that I am an instrument of Your peace.*

EJOICE always. . . .

—1 Thes 5:16

DEC. 31

REFLECTION. Freshen your New Year Resolutions with joy. We end the year where we began it, with the words of Pope John Paul II:

"Christ came to bring joy; joy to children, joy to parents, joy to families and to friends, joy to workers, and to scholars, joy to the sick and elderly, joy to all humanity. In a true sense, joy is the keynote message and the recurring motif of the Gospels. . . . Be messengers of joy."

PRAYER. *Thank You, Lord, for a grace-filled year. Thank You for the gift of joy.*

HOLY WEEK
PALM SUNDAY

 ND the crowds that went before Him, and those that followed, kept crying out, "Hosanna to the Son of David."

—Mt 21:9

REFLECTION. We are here to profess with victorious vigor that Christ is the Way, the Truth, and the Life.

The explosion of our faith is so strong that—as Jesus said—if our voice were to keep silence, the stones would cry out instead.   —*Pope Paul VI*

PRAYER. *Lord Jesus, the crowd cried out "Hosanna," which means, "Lord, save us." I also cry out today with my voice and my heart, "Hosanna, Son of David."*

HOLY THURSDAY

 OW that I, your Lord and Master, have washed your feet, you also ought to wash the feet of one another.

—Jn 13:14

REFLECTION. During the Eucharistic celebration there is the ceremony of the washing of feet. It was the custom to wash the feet of a guest in Jesus' time.

Today it is a sign of our willingness to love and care for our neighbor.

PRAYER. *Lord, make me willing to wash the feet of those who need my love.*

GOOD FRIDAY

 OD forbid that I should glory save in the Cross of our Lord Jesus Christ.

—Gal 6:14

REFLECTION. To glory in the Cross is not making the Cross an end in itself. The Lord did not die that our cross may be heavy. He died that our joy may be complete. St. Augustine said, "We are an Easter people and Alleluia is our song."

PRAYER. *Dear Jesus, there are no words to express my gratitude for Your love. Help me to see that the Cross is merely a means to an end. Teach me that joy is the end of all revelation.*

HOLY SATURDAY

 ECAUSE of the Preparation Day of the Jews, they laid Jesus in a new tomb in which no one had yet been laid.

—Jn 19:41-42

REFLECTION. The readings in the Paschal Vigil carry us into the mysterious arena where human sin meets God's justice and mercy.

There life and death "have contended," and there the victory of the risen Christ over death stands out as the source of our salvation and the model of Christian living. —*Pope Paul VI*

PRAYER. *This day is filled with silence, Lord, as we await the outpouring of joy with which we will celebrate Your Resurrection. Help me to prepare diligently for that great event.*

191

EASTER SUNDAY

GOD raised this Jesus to life. Of that we all are witnesses.

—Acts 2:32

REFLECTION. After the tragic death of Jesus, sadness covered the Holy Land. It lasted until the crack of dawn on Easter Sunday. Then a shout was heard around all of Jerusalem: He is risen! Jesus is risen from the dead!

To this very day the same cry of joy is heard around the world. ALLELUIA!

PRAYER. *Holy, holy, holy Lord, God Almighty. We joyfully proclaim Your Resurrection! Alleluia!*

PRAYER TO LIVE JOYFULLY

Lord, at times I am overcome with joy.
The world seems such a glorious place
and all the cares of life seem far away.
Thank You for giving us a glimpse of eternity.
I know that such a grand feeling is sure to pass
and that I will be once again confronted
with the problems and worries of daily life.
Let me realize that true joy never fades,
for it is the gift of Your Spirit
made possible by the saving action of Jesus.
Keep me in Your grace
so that I may never lose that inner virtue of joy.

OTHER OUTSTANDING BOOKS IN THIS SERIES

WORDS OF COMFORT FOR EVERY DAY—Short meditation for every day including a Scripture text and a meditative prayer to God the Father. Printed in two colors. 192 pages. **Ask for No. 186**

LEAD, KINDLY LIGHT—By Rev. James Sharp. Minute meditations for every day of the year taken from the writings of Cardinal Newman plus a concluding prayer for each day. **Ask for No. 184**

EVERY DAY IS A GIFT—Introduction by Most Rev. Frederick Schroeder. Popular meditations for every day, featuring a text from Sacred Scripture, a quotation from the writings of a Saint, and a meaningful prayer. **Ask for No. 195**

MARY DAY BY DAY—Minute meditations for every day of the year, including a Scripture passage, a quotation from the Saints, and a concluding prayer. Printed in two colors with over 300 illustrations. **Ask for No. 180**

MINUTE MEDITATIONS FROM THE POPES—By Rev. Jude Winkler, O.F.M. Conv. Minute meditations for every day of the year using the words of twentieth-century Popes. Printed and illustrated in two colors. **Ask for No. 175**

AUGUSTINE DAY BY DAY—By Rev. John Rotelle, O.S.A. Minute meditations for every day of the year taken from the writings of Augustine, with a concluding prayer also from the Saints. **Ask for No. 170**

BIBLE DAY BY DAY—By Rev. John Kersten, S.V.D. Minute Bible meditations for every day including a short Scripture text and brief reflection. Printed in two colors with 300 illustrations. **Ask for No. 150**

MINUTE MEDITATIONS FOR EACH DAY— By Rev. Bede Naegele O.C.D. This very attractive book offers a short Scripture text, a practical reflection, and a meaningful prayer for each day of the year. **Ask for No. 190**

LIVING WISDOM FOR EVERY DAY—By Rev. Bennet Kelley, C.P. Choice texts from St. Paul of the Cross, one of the true Masters of Spirituality, and a prayer for each day. **Ask for No. 182**

WHEREVER CATHOLIC BOOKS ARE SOLD